Do I Look at You with Love?

Personal/Public Scholarship

Series Editor

Patricia Leavy (*USA*)

VOLUME 9

Do I Look at You with Love?

Reimagining the Story of Dementia

By

Mark Freeman

BRILL
SENSE

LEIDEN | BOSTON

Cover illustration: Marian Freeman in her youth, circa 1942

All chapters in this book have undergone peer review.

The Library of Congress Cataloging-in-Publication Data is available online at
http://catalog.loc.gov

ISSN 2542-9671
ISBN 978-90-04-46058-4 (paperback)
ISBN 978-90-04-46059-1 (hardback)
ISBN 978-90-04-46060-7 (e-book)

ADVANCE PRAISE FOR
DO I LOOK AT YOU WITH LOVE?

"Written in a prose which is both scholarly and profoundly compassionate, Mark Freeman recounts the journey of his mother's dementia from a son's perspective, using insights gained from his years of thinking about how we come to tell the stories we live, what happens when those threads fall apart, and exploring what cultural tools are available to us to tell stories of decline and death. This book will bring fresh insights combined with a deep sense of recognition to anyone interested in questions of memory and identity, who has lived with someone with dementia, or even struggled with the gradual loss of a loved one. While the story told here is about a particular person, in a particular time and place, with a particular son, Freeman offers the reader a philosophical contemplation on the meaning of love and loss, inviting us to reflect on who we are in relation to others in our lives, and the trouble of making sense when those others can no longer be present."
– **Molly Andrews, Professor of Political Psychology and co-director, Centre for Narrative Research, University of East London, author of *Narrative Imagination* and *Everyday Life and Shaping History: Narratives of Political Change***

"Through his deep, intimate portrait of his relationship with his mother over more than a decade of dementia, Freeman investigates questions central to being human: How do we locate ourselves in space and time? Do we still have a self when we don't have our story? How do we discover our deepest level of connection to others? This engaging book gently challenges each of us to question our part in upholding society's disdain for aging, illness and death and digs to the bedrock of what is needed for us to be good to one another. In a humble yet scholarly manner, Freeman invites us to develop our own understandings through visiting with him and his beloved mother on her journey through dementia to death."
– **Susan Bluck, Professor of Psychology and Director, Life Story Lab, University of Florida**

"For more than thirty years, Mark Freeman's philosophically inspired contributions to narrative inquiry have widened and deepened our conceptual understanding of how stories work in and on our sense-making lives. In *Do I Look at You with Love?*, Freeman embarks on a different kind of inquiry, attempting to join his academic dexterity to his own (and his mother's) lived experience in order to reimagine dementia. The result is a daring, refreshing, and intimate portrait that merges the academic and the personal, the intellectual and the spiritual, the desire to make sense and the attentiveness to let go of the sense one has made. *Do I Look at You with Love?* is a gift that guides readers to a deeper understanding of the human condition, the sacred, and the unknown.

Freeman's most ingenious observations show how identities too often are imposed on us, requiring us to challenge the moral understanding and consequences of the stories, or fragments of story, that circulate widely in the community in which we find or locate ourselves. This makes the task of keeping the door open without expectations nearly impossible. We become entrapped by our own (or our culture's) story. Freeman shows the many ways in which the caregiver of a parent with dementia lives in a canonical story saturated with dread, terror, worry, and hopelessness. Typically, the parent is ill and the caregiver wounded. How then to care with compassion, patience, and generosity; with gentleness, humanity, and honesty; with loving kindness? Freeman approaches these questions by candidly fusing doubt and hope, seeking a story that might prepare future caregivers (and students of the human sciences) for both the perils and the joys lying ahead. Refusing to romanticize or revile, Freeman gradually recognizes that what may violate, deprive, or disrupt us may also bring us closer to the moral good and a capacity to 'be with' that validates the priority of the other and allows a measure of beauty and joy to arise. In the process, he shows us what it can mean for an academic and/or a caregiver to strive for an acute self-consciousness and an appropriately shameless subjectivity. This is Freeman's intellectual and spiritual gift to readers. *Do I Look at You with Love?* made me feel as if I was in conversation with another consciousness intent on feeling less alone and more human, and helping me, the reader, to feel that way as well. If this represents Freeman's goals for an artful human science, I am all in."

– Art Bochner, Distinguished University Professor Emeritus, University of South Florida, author of *Coming to Narrative: A Personal History of Paradigm Change in the Human Sciences* and co-author (with Carolyn Ellis), *Evocative Autoethnography: Writing Lives and Telling Stories*

"Not only does Mark Freeman honor his mother's memory with this remarkable book, he honors his readers by entrusting them with a self—and soul—searching account of his mother's last 12 years with dementia. He has managed to incorporate many aspects of his philosophical scholarship and understanding of narrative psychology into a work that reads like an intimate conversation, often poetic in its beauty. At the same time, perhaps because he emphasizes the irreducible uniqueness of his relationship with his mother, it seems impossible to read his book without asking questions about the meaning of love and finitude and relation to the Other in one's own life."
– **Doris Brothers, Psychologist/Psychoanalyst, author of** *Toward a Psychology of Uncertainty: Trauma-Centered Psychoanalysis* **and** *Falling Backwards: An Exploration of Trust and Self-Experience*

"Mark Freeman writes of his mother's dementia with a son's sharp wonderment and intimate sorrow. Layered over these, he offers a psychologist's search for understanding, a search that yields as many questions as answers. What is a self without memory, without narrative? Tracing the progression of his mother's loss, he discovers profound sweetness alongside the pain; moments of startling, salty humor; and eventually a kind of found poetry in their increasingly pared-down verbal exchanges, which read almost like nursery rhymes, full of puzzlement and beauty and love."
– **Leah Hager Cohen, James N. and Sarah L. O'Reilly Barrett Professor in Creative Writing, College of the Holy Cross, author of** *Strangers and Cousins* **and** *The Grief of Others*

"In *Do I Look at You with Love?*, Mark Freeman invites readers into his deep and complicated relationship with his mother as she moves through messy stages of Alzheimer's disease. As he bears witness to his mother's life—and his own—Mark rises to the needs of the situation by gradually giving himself over to the 'priority of the other.' Acknowledging both the terror and the joy of 'being with' his mother over years of her steady decline, Mark's love story evokes empathy and identification with the demands of a life circumstance akin to being held 'hostage.' The stories he tells about their time together evoke the tragic dimensions yet 'sacred beauty of finite life,' the sometimes quiet joy of cognitive decline, and the love and care between mother and son. The astute conceptual analysis of the stages she (and they) go through provide insight into the mortal reality of the life we all live. The ethical questions that arise lead to innovative thinking about our role as researchers and characters

in the personal stories we tell, and how we represent the 'other.' *Do I Look at You with Love?* is storytelling and analysis at its best, written by the most keenly observant and sensitive narrative psychologist of our time. Mark has accomplished his goal to 'memorize' his mother, and now this story lives with readers, no doubt moving us to do the same with our loved ones."
– **Carolyn Ellis, Distinguished University Professor Emerita, author of *Revision: Autoethnographic Reflections on Life and Work* and *Final Negotiations: A Story of Love, Loss, and Chronic Illness***

"Mark Freeman, a major thinker in narrative psychology, tells the story of his mother's evolving dementia with his penetrating mind and his expansive heart. As he struggles to stay emotionally connected to her, he analyzes with his penetrating insight, the role and limits of narrative in our lives. This beautifully written book is both moving and illuminating, a must-read for anyone who lives or works with people with dementia or any psychologist interested in how we are created by, but exist beyond, our life narratives."
– **Ruthellen Josselson, Professor of Clinical Psychology, Fielding Graduate University, author of *Narrative and Cultural Humility: Lessons from the "Good Witch" Teaching Psychotherapy in China* and *Paths to Fulfillment: Women's Search for Meaning and Identity***

"In 'memorizing' carefully the phases of his mother's journey with dementia, a journey he shared with her, Freeman draws on a wealth of insight into the links between memory, identity, and narrative to pen for us not just a moving tribute to what he calls dementia's 'tragic promise,' but also a deeply thoughtful meditation on the precious beauty of Life itself, in all its complexity and mystery, transiency and loss."
– **William Randall, Professor of Gerontology, St. Thomas University, author of *In Our Stories Lies Our Strength: Aging, Spirituality, and Narrative* and *The Narrative Complexity of Ordinary Life: Tales from the Coffee Shop***

In loving memory of my mother, Marian,
and loving gratitude for all of those who held
her during her final years

There's a crack in everything
That's how the light gets in
– Leonard Cohen, "Anthem"

CONTENTS

ACKNOWLEDGMENTS

For this project, I owe a great debt to those people I consider fellow travelers in inquiries of this sort—that is, inquiries into the lives of flesh and blood human beings, in the hope of learning something about them and about the human condition. These include Tony Adams, Molly Andrews, Michael Bamberg, Robert Bishop, Susan Bluck, Art Bochner, Jens Brockmeier, Doris Brothers, Carolyn Ellis, Michelle Fine, Roger Frie, Andy Futterman, David Goodman, Lars-Christer Hydén, Ruthellen Josselson, Suzanne Kirschner, Amia Lieblich, Jack Martin, Dan McAdams, Hanna Meretoja, Mary Beth Morrissey, Bill Randall, Frank Richardson, Brian Schiff, Brent Slife, Jeff Sugarman, and Jonathan Wyatt. In addition, I want to acknowledge some of my colleagues and friends at Holy Cross, especially Renee Beard, Leah Hager Cohen, Bob Cording, Margaret Freije, Osvaldo Golijov, Ed Isser, Jim Kee, Lynn Kremer, Vicki Swigert, Frank Vellaccio, Steve Vineberg, and Chick Weiss. I'm immensely grateful to them all, and also to the Department of Psychology and the College more generally for supporting the work I do as a teacher, scholar, and writer.

I also wish to acknowledge several intellectual communities that I have had the great good fortune of being a part of while writing this book, including the Philosophy Reading Group at Holy Cross; the Society for Personology, a group of scholars strenuously committed to exploring human lives in all their complexity and richness; the Narrative Study Group, coordinated and graciously sponsored for many years by Elliot Mishler; the Society for Qualitative Inquiry in Psychology; and the Psychology and the Other Institute, ably and imaginatively brought into being by David Goodman. How fortunate I've been to be in dialogue with the people in these groups, many of whom have become close and much-treasured friends.

This book is the product of many people associated with Brill | Sense. Special thanks to Patricia Leavy, whose creative, venturesome work as writer and editor have served to both widen and deepen the field of inquiry into the human experience; Shalen Lowell, for their good work shepherding this project through; John Bennett, for his enthusiastic encouragement and support of this and Jolanda Karada, for her helpful finishing touches. Thanks also go to Laurel Richardson, a kindred spirit I only recently met, whose own distinctive voice as a writer and scholar helped to convince me that Brill | Sense might make a good and appropriate home for a project of this sort, and Katie Lowery for her good and wise editorial eye.

Finally, I want to acknowledge and express my deep gratitude to my many and much-loved friends from back home who knew my mother well (you know who you are; I'm afraid to name you all lest I forget someone!); to my brothers, Bob and Ken, my sisters-in-law, Felice (Lissy) and Randy, and my nieces and nephews; and especially to my wife, Debbie, who loved and cared for my mother selflessly throughout the dementia years and beyond, our daughters, Brenna and Justine, who were with us and their beloved grandma every step of the way, and our son-in-law Matt, whose kindness and care were present throughout. They're all part of this book, and I'm grateful for their contributions and their presence in my life.

And of course, there's my mother, Marian Weiner Freeman. What to say? I couldn't have written this book without her! I think she'd like that sentence and sentiment. But she might have wanted me to say something more serious too. So I will: This book has been a labor of love, and I hope that my love for the person who inspired it is visible in all that follows.

***

Do I Look at You With Love? brings together much of the thinking and writing I did through the dozen years of my mother's dementia, and also moves significantly beyond it. Although none of the book's chapters reproduce in full the work that was published elsewhere, a number of them make significant contact with this earlier work. Articles and chapters drawn upon include, "Beyond Narrative: Dementia's Tragic Promise," in L.-C. Hydén & J. Brockmeier (Eds.), *Health, Illness, and Culture: Broken Narratives*, pp. 169–184 (Routledge, 2008); "Life without Narrative? Autobiography, Dementia, and the Nature of the Real," in G. O. Mazur (Ed.), *Thirty Year Commemoration to the Life of A. R. Luria*, pp. 129–144 (Semenko Foundation, 2008); "The Stubborn Myth of Identity: Dementia, Memory, and the Narrative Unconscious," *Journal of Family Life*, 2009, *1*; "From Absence to Presence: Finding Mother, Ever Again," in J. Wyatt and T. Adams (Eds.), *On (Writing) Families: Autoethnographies of Presence and Absence, Love and Loss*, pp. 49–56 (Sense Publishers, 2014); "Heeding the Face of the Other: A Case Study in Relational Ethics," *Human Arenas*, 2019, *1*; and "The Sacred Beauty of Finite Life: Re-imagining the Face of the Other," *Psychoanalytic Inquiry*, *40*, 161–172.

INTRODUCTION

A DIFFERENT KIND OF STORY

The words found in the title of this book were uttered by my mother, when she learned, once again, that I was her son.

***

This book explores the experience of dementia as it transpired during the course of the final 12 years of my mother's life, from the time of her diagnosis until her death in 2016 at the age of 93. As a longtime student of memory, identity, and narrative as well as the son of a woman with dementia, I had a remarkable opportunity to try to understand and narrate the trajectory of her experience. The process was difficult. The fact that she is my mother, and suffered, is one reason. Another is the fact that much of her experience remained obscure—I could only surmise the realities of her inner world. In addition, there was the challenge of narrative itself, of finding a way to tell her story that would truly do justice to her life. The fact that much of her story is tragic is clear enough. I won't be skating over these periods; they were extremely painful for her and for those of us who were entrusted with her care. Nor, however, will I focus solely on the challenges and heartbreaks. For there were other periods and other dimensions of relationship that were quite beautiful, and that could not have emerged without her very affliction. This is part of the story too. So it is that I have come to think of her story as a kind of "tragicomedy," one that is emblematic of nothing less than the bittersweet reality of life itself.

Paralleling each chapter of my mother's life during the period I explore were my own chapters, both lived and written. In speaking of the former, I am referring to my own experience as son and as narrative psychologist interested in memory and identity. In speaking of the latter, I am referring to the various articles, chapters, and presentations I crafted that sought to address my mother's situation, with special attention to the issue of narrative (e.g., Freeman, 2008a, 2008b, 2009, 2010a, 2014a). I draw significantly on these earlier works in this book. Now that my mother has passed, however, it is time to integrate the chapters of our shared lives into a larger story.

This larger story is but one story that might be told. The "life history" of dementia is not the same for everyone; for each and every person afflicted with the disease, there is a different story to be told, growing out of his or her unique history and character, the specific form the disease has assumed, the quality of the relationships able to be sustained, and more. I don't know that there were many comic stories to be told about the characters I encountered at the various places my mother lived, but there certainly seemed to be some flat-out tragedies: people who cried much of the day, or screamed in misery, or were wholly alone in their tortured worlds, day in and day out, for many years on end. I would never want to suggest, therefore, that the story I tell in this book is a story of "how it is." Rather, it's a story of how it was for this particular person, in this particular time and place, with this particular son.

The story I tell in this book wasn't the same for me across the years either, certainly not when my mother became a skipping record of pain, unable to be deterred from perseverating about her fate in utter confusion, and not when she had to be admitted to the geriatric psychiatry ward of a local hospital because the staff at her assisted living residence could no longer handle her. Were I to have told her story then, it would have been much closer to the flat-out tragedy her peers lived, a descent into a hellish void. In that scenario, I would have been little more than an impotent witness with virtually no power to shift the direction of things. As my mother's situation changed, so too did the stories I could tell.

I wasn't entirely sure which time frame to use in telling the story at hand. I could have merely reproduced the various pieces I wrote about my mother's life. I could have told the various stories as they had emerged at the time, as if I didn't know what would follow, how it all would end. But the fact is, I *do* know what followed, and I do know how it all ended. This knowledge is bound to influence the way I tell the story. To the greatest extent possible, however, I try to tell my mother's story in a way that both captures how things were at the time and avows the irretrievable fact of my telling this story now, in the present, looking back over the terrain of the past (see Freeman, 2010b). Along the lines being drawn, I employ what Phillip Lopate (2013) refers to as a "double perspective," one that seeks to keep in view "the experience as it was lived"—or told shortly after—while also benefiting from the more capacious perspective made available through narrative reflection.

I want to mention an issue related to the present endeavor. When I wrote about my mother's dementia in the aforementioned articles, chapters, and presentations, I generally steered clear of immersing myself in the relevant dementia literature—that is, the literature oriented toward the lived experience of *persons*. I am thinking here of the work of people like Anne Basting (2009), Lars-Christer Hydén (2017; see also Hydén, Lindemann, & Brockmeier, 2014), Tom Kitwood (1997), and Steven Sabat (2001; see also Hughes, Louw, & Sabat, 2006), work that explicitly addresses some of the issues I take up in my own writing. I avoided reading too broadly on the topic because I wanted to describe and reflect on what was going on as we actually lived it, and then fashion my own concepts and categories in response. These pieces had plenty of references, but they were more directed to the narrative and identity literature than to explicit treatments of dementia. In writing this book, I have adopted a similar strategy, staying with the relatively "naïve" viewpoint found in my earlier work, and generating my own concepts and categories accordingly. Given what I do know about the dementia literature, and given people's responses to my work, what I have to say here is in keeping with some of what's been said by others who have engaged in larger, more comprehensive research projects. Nevertheless, the ideas I fashion and the conclusions I ultimately draw derive mainly from what I learned firsthand as a philosophically oriented, narrative psychologist encountering new, uncharted experiential territory.

One additional qualification seems appropriate to offer before turning to some specifics. I am addressing but one "case" of dementia, and that particular case happens to be my mother, so it is not entirely clear to which genre of writing this book belongs. Although there is a good deal of psychological research on dementia, much of it is depersonalized, standard psychological fare. That sort of work has its place; it is important to know predictors, correlates, consequences, and so on. But with few notable exceptions, several of which I just cited, the dementia literature in psychology has focused more on the relevant variables and less on the lived experiences of persons. On the other end of the continuum of work on dementia (including Alzheimer's) is biographical work. There are extensive examples of this sort of work too (e.g., DeBaggio, 2002; Geist, 2008; Miller, 2003; Skloot, 2004; Whouley, 2011). But as valuable as that work may be for exploring the personal dimension, it generally stops short of providing the kinds of understandings and insights this book seeks to provide by virtue of my own background and expertise as a narrative psychologist interested in memory and identity who has been working in the field for close to 40 years. As far as I know, there is no work currently available that marries the academic and the personal, not, at least, in the narrative-psychological way I do in this book.

Bringing this book into being has thus been something of a high-wire act. By virtue of the nature of the project, the book doesn't fall readily into the usual categories. Is it a work of psychological science? According to most extant conceptions of science, no; it is too personal and idiosyncratic. Is it a work of psychological art? Is it a memoir? Those seem closer in some ways, but I am interested in speaking to more than this singular case (cautiously, of course). I do engage with important theoretical issues, and I draw some conclusions that I hope will prove relevant both to the study of dementia and to psychological inquiry more generally. This book is thus something of a hybrid, something between science, as traditionally conceived, and art. What to call it is largely immaterial in any case. The main thing is that it speak cogently to the realities being explored, and that it does so with a light enough touch to keep the book accessible, interesting, and humanly meaningful and relevant. The reader will of course be the best judge of the book's success in realizing these aims.

***

In Chapter 1, "A Relational Perspective on Dementia," I introduce my mother and myself and lay out the contours of the basic approach I take throughout the body of the book, which comprises the four subsequent chapters. In introducing my mother, I provide a brief sketch of her history and character until the time of her diagnosis. In introducing myself, I speak mainly to my work as a narrative psychologist with a special interest in memory, identity, and more recently, the place of the "Other" in the story of the self. My academic experience generally served me well in my efforts to make sense of the dozen or so years of my mother's dementia. At the same time, nothing can prepare a child for a parent's descent into this sort of affliction. This tension, between what I knew as a scholar and what I couldn't know, between "making sense" of things and letting that sense go, and, not least, between being a psychologist and being a son, permeates this chapter and the rest of the book. Indeed, I see this tension as one of the most distinctive features of the book.

In this introductory chapter, I also address the ethics of this project. My mother knew I was writing about her (early on), and was delighted ("My loving professor-son is writing about *me*!"). But she didn't fully understand what that meant, and agreeable though she was, she couldn't really give consent. As for the stories I have told and will be telling here, she couldn't possibly tell them; only I could. And I couldn't possibly tell them in a way that faithfully depicted her own "otherness." I often had no idea what her world was like, particularly in the later years. What does it mean to write about someone whose inner world may, in a very real sense, be unfathomable? There are also the ethics of portraying this story as something other than a flat-out tragedy and sometimes describing scenes that, on *some* level, are even humorous. Does doing so make light of what is a horrifyingly tragic experience through and through for many? Is it justifiable to call attention to episodes like these? I believe it is, but some rhetorical massaging will surely be required to make the case.

Chapter 2, titled "Protest," begins around the time of my mother's diagnosis, focusing mainly on her initial years at Tatnuck Park, an assisted living residence in Worcester, Massachusetts, where my family and I live. This phase was an extremely painful one, for my mother and for us. The reason, put in (too) simple terms, is that although she did have some awareness of her new "status," she never truly understood the changes she was going through; consequently, she protested mightily against her developing infirmities, against our own efforts to apprise her of her changing situation, and against the various prohibitions we had to put in place (driving, for instance) for her own safety and well-being.

In light of these issues, I put forth the idea of "deconstructing the cultural story" in the first piece I wrote about her (Freeman, 2008a), suggesting that a portion of my mother's response to her situation might plausibly be considered the "product of a culture that, in a distinct sense, refuses to admit the reality of decline, and death, into its midst." I also suggested the existence of a "dual narrative … operating behind the scenes of consciousness." First, there was "the narrative of the vital, self-sufficient Individual, who resists the kind of fragility, vulnerability, and dependency that growing old sometimes brings in tow" (p. 176). Second, there was what I called "the narrative of inexorable decline," which, in a distinct sense, operates in tandem with—and is on some level parasitic upon—the first. What I was seeing back then were the ways in which certain aspects of culturally rooted features of subjectivity—having to do with autonomy, self-sufficiency, the denial of death, and more—had become inscribed in my mother in such a way as to render her life extremely frustrating and painful. I so wished that she could let some of those features go. In fact, I tried to help her in this by offering some counter-narratives—for instance, about vulnerability and dependency and fragility, how these were okay. They never quite took. Hence, the depth of her protest. It was in this first phase, especially, that I saw the "underside" of narrative, the way in which one could become entrapped by one's own story.

Chapter 3, "Presence," explores a correlation I began to see as time went by, one that in its own tragic way promised a measure of reprieve, both for my mother and for those of us entrusted with her care: The more her ego was on the line, the more painful things would be; her much-prized sense of autonomy and self-sufficiency were under attack. Conversely, the more her ego was muted—for instance, listening to music, going for a beautiful fall drive, going out for a nice dinner—the more at home in the world she would be. It was around this time that I realized that as her dementia "got worse," she would likely feel less tortured by her life. I even entertained the idea that she might be able to achieve a kind of mystical union, what I referred to as "dementia's tragic promise" (2008a): Owing to her continuing demise, I had ventured, my mother might have an unprecedented opportunity to be truly *present* to reality. It would, of course, be a quite different path to the kind of selflessness frequently associated with meditation, mindfulness practices, and so on—a kind of crash course, you could say—but it would be no less ecstatic for all that. Or so it seemed. Is it possible I elevated some of this, made it seem a bit "happier" than it was? Possibly. It's important, I believe, to try to discern one's own motives in this kind of situation.

In some ways, this chapter also speaks to the underside of narrative: Freed momentarily from the kinds of demands that narratives may impose (such as those culturally rooted demands for autonomy and self-sufficiency that will have been addressed in the previous chapter), one may indeed live more freely and in the moment. In this respect, the "loss" of narrative, dreadful though its source is, may actually yield some positive consequences. Living more in the moment was one. There was also a diminution of filters during this phase; while listening to some good music at a local concert venue one warm summer night, for instance, my mother all but danced in the aisles, free of the usual prohibitions and inhibitions. So it was, I had confessed one time (Freeman, 2008b), that for a fleeting moment (which I describe in this chapter), I *envied* her—so carefree, so uninhibited, so blessedly bereft of the oppressive weight of the world's demands. These ideas need to be put forth cautiously. This is because the loss of narrative, far from necessarily leading to the kind of carefree immersion in the world my mother had sometimes experienced, can also lead to the void.

Chapter 4, "Dislocation," picks up where Chapter 3 leaves off. Whatever envy I may have had during the phase just described was cast aside later that year. Instead of the seemingly selfless state of abandon that would sometimes come her way, my mother frequently experienced a kind of existential "dislocation," such that everything would become utterly alien to her. And instead of a quasi-mystical state of union, she would become fragmented, wondering not only where she was and how she might have gotten there, but who she was. During this phase, she was generally okay when she woke up each morning; the routines began and she could make her way through them without getting too disturbed. But she would sometimes wake up from her afternoon nap to find herself completely lost, scared and panicky. It was around this time that I would sometimes get a call at work. She had to speak to me, *now*. Debbie, my wife, or I had to drive over to see her, be there in the flesh. I wasn't just a caregiver at this phase. Oftentimes, I was nothing short of a lifeline, her sole connection to reality, and she clung to me for dear life. Leaving to go home or back to work had always been difficult, but it was exceptionally hard during this phase. On a good day, I am sure it didn't matter much to her: out of sight, out of mind. But I know that on other days, she felt abandoned and alone again, without any touchstones, any real connections to the world. I shudder to think about it, even now.

There is much to be learned from this phase too. The loss of narrative that had emerged through my mother's momentary immersions into the world was not experienced as loss; that is, there was no *felt* loss, no sense of what was missing. During this later phase, however, the loss had become palpable, and would sometimes eventuate in utter terror—the terror of at once knowing that something was profoundly wrong and not knowing quite what. I therefore learned that although life itself may not be as narrative-laden as some theorists (Bruner, 1987a) have suggested, life *without* narrative, without some sense of location or anchorage in one's history and story, could be extremely disturbing. Sometimes it was terrifying. Other times it led to shame; she would speak of being "brainless," "mindless," "like a child." During this phase, my mother's identity had largely become a negative one, tied to what she no longer was. There was no longer the kind of protest there had been earlier; there was confusion and lamentation and mourning over what had clearly and irrevocably been lost. There was also some significant perseveration during this phase, manifested in incessant questions about where she was, how she got there, why she was there, how long she had been there, and so on. I would divert her attention as best I could. When that proved to be impossible, she would have to go to the aforementioned geriatric psychiatry ward, in the hope that her pain and confusion could somehow be lessened. Rough, very.

Chapter 5 is titled "Release." As I had predicted in the first piece I wrote, where I identified dementia's tragic promise, things would eventually change for the better, at least subjectively. My mother moved to the Jewish

Healthcare Center in Worcester, where she lived for some six years, and owing to the progression of her disease, she moved beyond the kind of panic and confusion just described. Seen from the outside, her situation was bleak. In addition to dementia, she had Chronic Obstructive Pulmonary Disease (COPD), she needed a wheelchair, her paper-thin skin was mottled and black and blue, and she was virtually blind. Moreover, she had lost her sense of location entirely (she never knew she had moved to a nursing home), and as the years progressed, she had only the most minimal sense of her own history and identity, as well as mine. This meant that we often needed to get reacquainted when I went to see her; she would want to know who I was, whether I was married, had children, and so on. She wasn't pained to learn these fundamental facts about her own son; she was mainly curious, surprised, and glad to know that my family and I seemed to be nice.

My mother couldn't say much about her life during this phase, not explicitly at any rate. That requires a well-stocked memory, a past, and some way of synthesizing things, of bringing one's experiences into connection in some way. Nevertheless, there was still a sense that my presence seemed to mean something to her, something that somehow touched upon who she was and what she had been. There would often be a little surge of confusion when I got up to leave; she would wonder whether she was supposed to leave too. More often, though, there would be gratitude. I don't want to call us "lucky"; that would be stretching things. But the fact is that we shared a lot of time together and moments of intimacy of a sort we almost certainly wouldn't have had if she hadn't fallen victim to this disease. There were some light and funny moments during this phase too, especially during the many reacquaintances we went through. I share such episodes and more throughout this chapter. Far along in her dementia though she was at this phase, our time together was often sweet. I'm sure the rest of my family would say the same.

I need to proceed cautiously in this chapter and be mindful of those readers whose cherished family and friends afflicted with dementia weren't quite as "agreeable" as my mother had been. I don't want to sugarcoat things. Occasionally, there would be another bout of painful confusion, and sometimes, when people tried to rouse her in the mornings, she would become aggressive and strike out at them. All things considered, however, her final years were pretty good ones, if by "good" is meant a life relatively devoid of excessive suffering, sometimes punctuated by moments of human connection and pleasure. As for me and my family, we did what we could to simply *be* with her and bring her these kinds of moments. It may be shocking to hear, but in many ways, these later years were a gift.

Chapter 6 carries the somewhat audacious title, "Death, Dementia, and the Face of the Divine." Some of those who study persons with dementia seek to move beyond deficit language and conceptualizations, and wish to call attention to both the insufficiently acknowledged resources such persons frequently have and the ways in which relational "adjustments" can serve to sustain their dignity and sense of themselves as persons. This is important work, to be sure. I come at the issues at hand from a somewhat different perspective. For me, and for most of those who bear witness to their loved ones' descent into dementia, there is no questioning the very real deficits that may emerge, and no getting around the tragic dimension of the situation. I do speak to this tragic dimension and try my best to do so in a way that honors its existential meaning and significance. This means speaking about vulnerability and frailty and mortality, and doing so as forthrightly as I can. It also means speaking about the possible beauty of these very conditions—the "sacred beauty of finite life," as I put it in a recent article (Freeman, 2020a)— and thereby reimagining what might otherwise appear as either a horrific tale of dreadful decline or a valiant, even comic, tale of resourcefulness and resilience. In my experience, it is neither of these. Or at least, it was neither of these for my family and me. It was just life, with its ebbs and flows, its horrors and its wondrous deliverances, its assaults and its gifts. The story of dementia is a *human* story, replete with all the pain and pleasure the human story inevitably brings. This, at any rate, is how I tell it.

I close the book with a brief coda titled, "Reimagining Dementia, Reimagining Life." In it, I review some of the central themes of the preceding chapters and draw out some larger ideas about dementia and the human condition more generally. So often, people who knew about our situation would say things like, "Oh, what a burden you must be carrying," or, "How hard this must be for you. I'm so sorry." Sure, there were difficult times. But my family and I never felt that caring for my mother was a burden. So we'd often say something like, "Not really. It's just life." That's what it was for us. Life changed, in a way that was unexpected and unbidden. Sometimes that would lead to pain and sorrow. Often, though, it led to a sense of quiet joy, along with a newfound appreciation for all that life can be.

CHAPTER 1

A RELATIONAL PERSPECTIVE ON DEMENTIA

It was difficult to decide how to write this book, for some obvious reasons. The "protagonist" is my mother, and it was difficult to determine what sort of story to tell and what sort of genre was most appropriate. The challenge would have been great no matter who the protagonist was—a research subject, for instance, I might have gotten to know over a sizable period of time. A relationship would have formed; I would no doubt have come to care for him or her in some way, and as a consequence, I would surely have had to abandon whatever pretenses to "objectivity" I might have had. But none of this compares to the challenge of writing about my *mother*, and on some level, of course, me. Not surprisingly, there were times when I had to ask: Should I even be *doing* this? Won't I be "using" her in some way by writing about her? And if I go ahead with the project, how will my own relationship with her—my own needs, wishes, and dark corridors—enter the picture? Could I even *know* this? Why write this book anyway?

I had to. Actually, let me correct that. I didn't have to write this book, but I did have to write the various pieces of the book, which essentially comprise the various chapters of her dementia, from its onset to the end, over the dozen-year span of time in question. As my mother's son, the youngest of three, and very close to her (she moved to Worcester to be near me and my family well before the onset of the disease), I was, first and foremost, terribly saddened and upset by what was going on. Here was a smart, vibrant, attractive woman, in the process of being laid low. And again, here was my *mother*, whose grace and kindness and wisdom were in the process of being undermined and diminished. It was hard.

It was also fascinating at times. I say this with full acknowledgment of the fact that some readers may find this confession startling and possibly off-putting. "It's your *mother*, for God's sake!" they might say. "Put it *away*!" One of my closest friends said something to this effect early on, seeing it as part of a pattern that she couldn't quite fathom. She had referred to my unusual capacity to "objectify" what was going on in my life. I sensed both admiration in her words—for my ability to build a bridge between my life and my work, as well as repulsion—for what may have seemed like a voyeuristic venture out of bounds. When things happened in my family, or with a friend, or when I encountered something going on in the proverbial "real world" that led me into reflection, I would write about it. As a longtime student of narrative, with abiding interests in memory, identity, the life story, and related issues, it was second nature for me to do so. I was, I am, a writer. My friend, on the other hand, was much more the dispassionate empirical researcher, who prided herself on the kind of objectivity generally sought in social science and who, in addition, tended to see her academic work and her life as separate enterprises. So this was part of it. But the sheer fact that I was exploring and writing about my mother also made her uncomfortable.

I am quite sure she wasn't alone in feeling this way. In fact, I know she wasn't. That's because I myself was sometimes uncomfortable doing what I was doing. At some point during the early years of my mother's dementia, she would say something that I found poignant or profound, and I would take out my cell phone and type it out. Should I be doing that? Should I really be taking a brief time-out from being her son so I could preserve her, and sometimes my, words? And should I eventually try to take all of these "data" and form them into stories for conferences and journals and books? About midway through our journey together, I did this much more often, partly because I'd grown more comfortable doing it and partly because, in the later years especially, she more frequently uttered words that struck me as unusually interesting or profound or just plain weird. "I need to get that down," I'd say. I avow it. I *did* need to do that, and I'm glad I did. They're memorial treasures, and they've helped remind me of what life was truly like at the time. So, challenging though it was to be a … son/researcher (?), I believe it was a worthwhile endeavor.

Also challenging was the fact that my mother couldn't really consent to what I was doing—not, at least, in the informed consent mode of most social science. As noted earlier, I did tell her what I was doing. And in true mother (or at least *my* mother) fashion, she seemed delighted by it. "Ma," I might say, "as you know, I've been thinking and writing about people's lives for a long time, focusing on topics like memory and self. Some of what you're experiencing now is actually pretty relevant to my work. Is it okay if I share some things about you and your experience in my writing?"

"Of course you can write about me!" she would say.

She had only the most minimal idea of what I would write about. In fact, she had only the most minimal idea that she had fallen victim to dementia. The day she was diagnosed with Alzheimer's, she sobbed. That night, however, she had no memory at all of having been diagnosed or even having been to a doctor. During the early years, she knew that things were amiss. She also knew that Tatnuck Park wasn't just for "senior living," but for those who, in some way or another, had significant physical or mental needs. Remarkably enough, she quickly reached a point in which she had virtually no knowledge that she was afflicted with dementia. Does it matter that she would become the subject of my musings with nary a clue of what the substance of these musings were? And now that she is gone, does it matter that the final years of her life are the focus of a book? There have been times through the years when I felt that I was somehow taking advantage of her situation. One could argue that I am doing so right now, in this very book. This is surely true on some level. What exactly justifies it? Anything?

I discuss these issues in greater detail in the pages to follow. I should note that this chapter seeks to offer something of a philosophical and methodological framework for undertaking the present inquiry. As such, there are more academic references than in the other chapters, and the writing is, at times, somewhat denser and more formal. Some readers, especially those looking to situate their work in the context of philosophical and methodological discussions regarding person-oriented inquiry into dementia, will likely find this chapter, or portions of it, useful. On the other hand, those seeking to get to the heart of the story more quickly can safely skip over this chapter and move on to the subsequent one, which I consider the beginning of the body of the book. For now, I will simply say that if there is anything that justifies my writing—and your reading—this book, it is that it's a labor of love, born out of the abiding love I have for my mother (it's still very much there even if she is not) and out of the commitment I made, years ago, to tell her story in such a way that she might "live on the page" and thereby provide an account of dementia that moved beyond those more dispassionate—and in some instances, depersonalized—accounts one tends to find in much of the extant literature.

***

I begin with what may initially seem like a curious assertion: In exploring the process of relating to and caring for a loved one with dementia, we have in hand a potential model not only for practicing what is sometimes referred to as "relational research ethics," but also for human relations more generally. Please understand, I am not elevating myself as a model, as some sort of selfless, heroic caregiver. On the contrary, there were numerous times, in the early years especially, when I was anything but that, when I was frustrated, preoccupied with this or that, eager to flee. This changed in time. As I would eventually learn, being truly present to my mother meant living what I have elsewhere referred to as "the priority of the Other" (Freeman, 2014a). It meant being called out of myself, setting my own needs and preoccupations aside, and giving myself over to her. This meant learning how to truly pay attention, which, as Iris Murdoch (1970) has put it, entails nothing less and nothing more than "a just and loving gaze directed upon an individual reality" (p. 34).

Directing this gaze upon a person with dementia unquestionably entails a level of attention and compassion that may not be as readily realized in other relations. These other relations may not call us out of ourselves to the same degree or with the same intensity. That's to be expected. Nevertheless, bearing in mind the kind and quality of attention of which Murdoch and others (e.g., Weil, 1951/1973, 1952/1997) have spoken, we might think of the comparatively unalloyed attention that may emerge in encountering the person with dementia—or persons with other afflictions, demanding in their own ways—as a kind of regulative ideal or form, never to be fully realized but always something for which to strive.

I learned that my mother had been stricken with dementia 16 years ago. The tentative diagnosis was Alzheimer's disease, but because the disease could only be confirmed with a postmortem examination, those of us who spoke to her situation in the years that followed would generally refer to the more nonspecific "dementia." The diagnosis hit us hard. This, however, was a most unusual opportunity, irrevocably personal though it was. I had to see whether we all might learn something from her experience, something that might shed new and different light on the disease. For the time being, I simply note that this particular undertaking, such as it was, taught me more about relational research ethics, and indeed about relationality, than any other research endeavor I had ever pursued.

Some aspects of this mode of ethical thinking and practice may be traced back to my own and others' work in narrative psychology, which, broadly speaking, seek to explore *persons*—more specifically, the stories of persons' lives—rather than those "variables" that are at the heart of so much traditional psychological research, and to do so precisely through the kind of relationality that emerges in the context of in-depth interviews and the like (Freeman, 1993, 1997a; Josselson, 2006; Schiff, 2018). However, my main philosophical inspiration for much of my thinking about research ethics and relationality are the works of Martin Buber and Emmanuel Levinas, the latter of whose reflections on the priority of the Other have provided a broad ethical framework for carrying out my responsibilities as both scholar and, more importantly, son. Before turning to my mother's story, which is in part my own owing to the very relationality at hand, it may first be useful to share some additional words regarding my turn to a relational perspective on inquiry, and then, a brief sketch of Buber's and Levinas's ideas as they pertain to relational research ethics.

***

Like most scholars in the social sciences, much of the research I pursued, especially early in my career, assumed the traditional form of developing an interest, formulating hypotheses or conjectures about what I might discover through my efforts, carrying out the required work, and ultimately, writing it up in some meaningful way. Even then, I found myself attracted to a relational view of research. When I joined a large research project at the University of Chicago in the early 1980s, my advisors had been hopeful that I would be able to shed some of my humanistic impulses (and distaste for what I perceived to be the objectifying crudeness of much empirical research, especially in psychology) and carry out the more dispassionate, quantitatively oriented work they had been reared to value. Unfortunately (for them), the beautifully designed questionnaire that was to be distributed to our research participants during the first wave of the research left me cold. When our research team began poring over large stacks of green and white computer printouts and trying to determine where nodes of "significance" might be on the basis of the numbers and asterisks at hand ($p < .05!$), I found myself downright mystified. Somehow, this process and the inevitably ad hoc speculation it generated was seen to be in the service of objectivity. "We're not even talking with them!" I (essentially) said. "How are we supposed to understand who they are and what they're saying?" The answer, again: The t-tests and correlation matrices will tell us. Some people seemed positively enchanted with this process; for them, it was like mining for gold or precious jewels. They might also have enjoyed flexing their interpretive muscles in the face of the statistical findings, seeing whether they could tell some kind of story. It was rather like reading tea leaves.

Fortunately, the second wave of the project involved actual stories, which emerged from intensive life history interviews that would take me and others to lots of interesting places and that gave me some measure of entry into a more relational perspective. I still came in armed with questions (one project member needed me to ask question X for her dissertation, another needed me to ask question Y, and so on), but I was able to ask them in a relatively unstructured and open way in the context of an extended dialogue. I can't say I was entirely comfortable, even with this more open format. Partly because our research participants were aspiring artists, many of whom didn't much care for being interrogated about their art and creative process, and partly because I found the entire exercise to be intrusive and objectifying (gentle though my research touch tried to be), I eventually came to feel that I wasn't cut out for empirical research of this sort. On some level, the research endeavor seemed to me to be inherently objectifying, owing to the simple fact that I was there to get something from the people in question, something that ultimately had more to do with me and my interests than with them and theirs. I guess this is all but inevitable in any endeavor that entails research "on" this or that phenomenon, however "with" people one may aspire to be. Regardless, it didn't sit well with me.

On a more positive note, I grew to love the more theoretical and philosophical side of inquiry, and under the guidance of some stellar mentors, especially the philosopher Paul Ricoeur, I began to carry out work in narrative psychology, most of which focused on the interpretation of texts (e.g., Freeman, 1993, 1997b). Much of this work was theoretical in focus, drawing on interpretation theory and narrative theory as vehicles for exploring lives and life histories, but some was also directed to specific literary texts—memoirs and autobiographies especially—that could provide the kind of "data" I was most interested in exploring. I suppose one could say that this latter work was empirical in nature, focused as it was on particular lives, but certainly not in the way most social science conceived it. Not surprisingly, some of my colleagues in my home department began to wonder why I still called myself a psychologist (see Freeman, 2014b). I don't know that I ever provided answers that were satisfactory to them. So it goes. I'll be retiring soon.

Formative though this more literary approach to inquiry was, it certainly wasn't "relational" in nature, at least not in the way that the term is generally used in the context of research. The good news is that this work allowed me, and still allows me, to connect with important, real-life, human issues without feeling the unease I had felt when carrying out more traditional empirical research. At the same time, I eventually found myself inclined to make more contact with human issues as they emerged in the context of my life and the lives of those around me. So it was that I did a piece on a friend and colleague who was facing some severe challenges in his family's well-being (Freeman, 1999), one on the death of my father and its aftermath (Freeman, 2002a), another that explored a life-changing experience of my own during a visit to Berlin (Freeman, 2002b), and a more summative one that proclaimed (and was titled) "Data are Everywhere," the subtitle of which was, "Narrative Criticism in the Literature of Experience" (Freeman, 2003). It was in this piece that I sought to bring the approach I had adopted in relation to literary texts to the lives of real people, including my own. I have come to identify this mode of inquiry as "narrative hermeneutics" (Freeman, 2015a), and its most fundamental philosophical and methodological commitment is to practice fidelity—phenomenological and ethical—to these lives and the stories that issue from them.

During this phase of my work, I was certainly gesturing in the direction of a more explicitly relational approach to inquiry, but I hadn't quite arrived there. In the case of my colleague and friend, I mainly observed what was going on in his life, and with his permission, wrote about it. For the piece on my father, it was relational insofar as it drew on our lives prior to his death, but given that the piece in question was written some 25 years later, I hesitate to call it relational in the living sense that most relational research posits. As for the life-changing experience in Berlin I had written about, it was largely a "private" one that explored the depths of my own interior, and while other people were part of the story I would eventually tell, they really didn't figure prominently.

It wasn't until the onset of my mother's dementia that I began to move more squarely in the direction of a relational approach to research. I didn't intend to do so. I approached my mother as a son, not a researcher. This was so until her death, 12 years later. But as a narrative psychologist interested in people's lives, I wasn't one to ignore what I was seeing before me. Painful though aspects of those years were, I was fascinated at times too. I was learning things about memory and identity, in her life, in mine, and in our relationship, that I could never have learned otherwise. We also felt things we never would have felt. There were times, in fact, when it seemed as if entirely new regions of being had been opened up, owing to the very intimacy of our evolving relationship. I know some people were taken aback by my decision to write about all of this, but for me, it didn't feel like a decision at all. I had to do it. And in the process, I came to learn a good deal more about what relational research ethics might entail.

***

According to Buber (1970), there are two basic modes of encountering the world, both human and non-human. One is the "I-It" mode, found whenever and wherever we take an objectifying stance to the reality before us. In encountering a tree, for instance, "I can accept it as a picture ... I can assign it to a species and observe it as an instance, with an eye to its construction and way of life ... I can dissolve it into a number, into a pure relation between numbers, and externalize it. Throughout all of this," Buber explains, "the tree remains my object and has its place and its time span, its kind and condition" (pp. 57–58).

> But it can also happen, if will and grace are joined, that as I contemplate the tree I am drawn into a relation, and the tree ceases to be an It. The power of exclusiveness has seized me.
>
> This does not require me to forego any of the modes of contemplation. There is nothing that I must not see in order to see, and there is no knowledge that I must forget. Rather is everything, picture and movement, species and instance, law and number included and inseparably fused.
>
> Whatever belongs to the tree is included: its form and its mechanics, its colors and its chemistry, its conversation with the elements and its conversation with the stars—all this in its entirety. (p. 58)

This is the I-You mode, sometimes framed as the I-Thou mode, and it is based fundamentally on relation.

Much the same state of affairs emerges in encountering people, including those who may be the "objects" of our research. As Buber explains,

> When I confront a human being as my You and speak the basic word I-You to him, then he is no longer a thing among things nor does he consist of things. He is no longer He or She, limited by other Hes and Shes, a dot in the world grid of space and time, nor a condition that can be experienced and described, a loose bundle of named qualities ...
>
> Even as a melody is not composed of tones, nor a verse of words, nor a statue of lines—one must pull and tear to turn a unity into a multiplicity—so it is with the human being to whom I say You. I can abstract from him the color of his hair or the color of his speech or the color of his graciousness; I have to do this again and again; but immediately he is no longer You. (p. 59)

As Buber goes on to suggest, the I-You mode of relationality being considered is primary, in the sense of preceding the more objectifying I-It mode. As such, "We may suppose that relations and concepts, as well as the notions of persons and things, have gradually crystallized out of notions of relational processes and states" (p. 70). Along the lines being drawn here, adopting a relational research ethics entails a measure of "return" to a more primordial mode of encountering others, one that is more holistic, syncretistic, and respectful of the other's integrity. As Buber puts the matter in another important text, *Between Man and Man* (1965),

> This person is other, essentially other than myself, and this otherness of his is what I mean, because I mean him; I confirm it; I wish his otherness to exist, because I wish his particular being to exist …. That the men with whom I am bound up in the body politic and with whom I have directly or indirectly to do, are essentially other than myself, that this one or that one does not have merely a different mind, or way of thinking or feeling, or a different conviction or attitude, but has also a different perception of the world, a different recognition and order of meaning, a different touch from the regions of existence, a different faith, a different soil: to affirm all this, to affirm it in the way of a creature, in the midst of the hard situations of conflict, without relaxing their real seriousness, is the way by which we may officiate as helpers in this wide realm entrusted to us as well, and from which alone we are from time to time permitted to touch in our doubts, in humility and upright investigation, on the other's "truth" or "untruth," "justice" or "injustice." (pp. 61–62)

On this account, we must somehow deepen our attention to and regard for the other in his or her otherness, his or her differentness. We must, in fact, "affirm all this," take it to heart. Recognition is not enough; there needs to be care as well.

Of special importance in Buber's philosophy is the idea of the "between," which he (1965) considers "a primal category of human reality." As he explains, "The view which establishes the concept of 'between' is to be acquired by no longer localizing the relation between human beings, as is customary, either within individual souls or in a general world which embraces and determines them, but in actual fact between them." For Buber, therefore, "'Between' is not an auxiliary construction, but the real place and bearer of what happens between men" (p. 203). In sum, "On the far side of the subjective, on this side of the objective, on the narrow ridge, where I and Thou meet, there is the realm of 'between'" (p. 204; see also Gergen, 2009, on "relational being").

It should be noted that Buber is not addressing the research relationship here. Rather, he is speaking more generally of human relatedness, and issuing a call, as it were, for the kind of abiding-with that preserves the integrity of the other person in his or her uniqueness and differentness. This caveat aside, Buber's perspective bespeaks what Josselson (2006) has called an "ethical attitude" that is surely transportable to the research situation. At the center of Josselson's perspective is the importance of the researcher's being in an "appropriately respectful" relationship with the participant. More specifically, "ethical practice and ethical codes rest on the principles of assuring the free consent of participants to participate, guarding the confidentiality of the material, and protecting participants from any harm that may ensue from their participation" (p. 537). As Josselson adds, focusing on her own area of narrative research, "Ethics in narrative research ... is not a matter of abstractly correct behavior but of responsibility in human relationship" (p. 538). But what exactly is the responsibility being considered? First and foremost, it would seem, it would involve minimizing harm, and bespeaks the kind of "procedural ethics" that are part and parcel of Institutional Research Boards (IRBs) and the like. This commitment to minimizing harm is surely a necessary criterion for theorizing a relational research ethics. However, it may not be a sufficient one. The question then is: How else might we think about the issue of responsibility in the context of the research situation?

According to Ellis (2007), alongside procedural ethics, "the kind mandated by Institutional Review Board (IRB) committees to ensure procedures adequately deal with informed consent, confidentiality, rights to privacy, deception, and protecting human subjects from harm," there is what she (drawing on Guillemin & Gillam, 2004) refers to as "ethics in practice, or situational ethics, the kind that deal with the unpredictable, often subtle, yet ethically important moments" that emerge when, for instance, "someone discloses something harmful, asks for help, or voices discomfort with a question or her or his own response" (p. 4). Important though these two forms of ethics are in the research context, there is, finally, "relational ethics," which, in Ellis's view, is closely tied to the "ethics of care" put forth by Gilligan (1982), Noddings (1984), and others, and which "recognizes and values mutual respect, dignity, and connectedness between researcher and researched, and between researchers and the communities in which they live and work" (p. 4). Gergen, Josselson, and I have adopted a related stance in our (2015) discussion of "understanding with." Generally speaking, we offer, "psychologists have drawn a sharp distinction between the observing scientist and the subjects of observation," aiming "to observe with dispassion, and avoid personal relations with those we study." Important though this orientation may sometimes be, it "favors an analytic stance in which observing, categorizing, and counting are primary," with the result that the subjects at hand are transformed into the objects of our own dispassionate gaze. With the rise of certain strands of qualitative inquiry, there has, in contrast, emerged "an abiding sense that our knowledge is not about you, but with you. Rather than playing cat and mouse," therefore, "science and society collaborate in the search for understanding" (p. 7).

As one of the authors of this article, suffice it to say that I concur with most of it! At the same time, I find myself questioning some aspects of it. One question is whether a truly relational research ethics ought to be situated under the umbrella of "science." There are political reasons for doing so, of course. Foremost among them is the fact that the discourse of science and scientificity remains dominant in psychology and allied disciplines. For the most part, therefore, I have sought in my own work to adopt the relevant language, the goal essentially being to render the idea of science more capacious than it tends to be (e.g., Freeman, 2011). In recent years, however, I have come to question this very commitment and have begun to wonder whether the kind of ethics being sought requires other, perhaps more artful modes of inquiry altogether (e.g., Freeman, 2015b, 2018, 2020b).

The other question that surfaces, especially in view of the idea of "understanding with," concerns these very words: "understanding" and "with." Understanding others, in the research situation and beyond, is surely a worthy goal, but it may not be the main goal. And in the case of a phenomenon such as dementia, it may not be a feasible one. Could I really "understand" my mother during the final leg of her affliction with dementia? Was that even something to aspire to? As for understanding with her, that was well beyond the scope of my "research." Actually, was I even engaged in research? For me, at any rate, this is another one of those words that doesn't quite fit with the broadly relational view I have come to adopt. Could it be that the very idea of a relational research ethics is questionable? Do the words "relational," "research," and "ethics" really work together?

Let me not quibble too much about these words, loaded though they are. "Relational research ethics," Ellis (2007) tells us, "requires researchers to act from our hearts and minds" and "to acknowledge our interpersonal bonds to others" (p. 4). Moreover, Josselson (2006) had said, such an ethics is fundamentally about "responsibility in human relationship" (p. 538). As already noted, minimizing harm to those we study is certainly part of the picture. Nevertheless, I ask again: How else might we think about the issue of responsibility in the context of the research situation? Josselson herself

21

provides some helpful clues in her discussion of benefits accruing from the research. "Those who argue for explicit benefits to participants are working in a social justice framework, hoping that their work will lead to empowerment of the participants and/or the group they represent and also engender better societal treatment of those whom they study. Those working from a basic science stance," on the other hand, "implicitly assume that greater knowledge of human experience will lead to a more humane society" (2006, p. 555).

These are valuable benefits, to be sure, and do well to move the idea of responsibility beyond that of minimizing harm. But there is still more. Whatever benefits may accrue from our research, there remains the issue of what was earlier referred to by Josselson as an "ethical attitude." This attitude "involves deep contemplation about what it means to encounter and represent 'otherness.'" Such an attitude also "mandates that the researcher question personal assumptions about the normal, healthy, or desirable" (p. 555). Taking these two aspects of the ethical attitude together, through the lens of narrative hermeneutics, research ethics has, as its first and most fundamental commitment, a stance of radical openness and receptivity to what is other.

With these last ideas, we return to Buber's (1965) reflections on the I-Thou relationship. "This person" before me, he had said, "is other, essentially other than myself," and "does not have merely a different mind, or way of thinking or feeling, or a different conviction or attitude, but has also a different perception of the world, a different recognition and order of meaning, a different touch from the regions of existence, a different faith, a different soil" (pp. 61–62). This difference is not only to be recognized, but affirmed and respected. An important if somewhat paradoxical qualification needs to be made in this context—namely, that this dimension of difference being considered has as its counterpart a kind of intimacy owing to the shared humanness involved. As I have put the matter elsewhere (Freeman, 2014a), however readily we might engage in dialogical relations with the other-than-human world, "there is no dialogue quite like the one we can have with another human being, and there is no 'You' quite like the one that assumes the form of the living, breathing person, standing before us" (p. 84). One very basic reason is that other persons "talk back" to us in a way that is, by all appearances, unparalleled. Amidst difference, therefore, is a measure of sameness and familiarity. Another, related reason is that this talking-back bears within it a dimension of reciprocity. "Relation is reciprocity. My You acts on me as I act on it. Our students teach us, our works form us …. Inscrutably involved, we live in the currents of universal reciprocity" (Buber, 1970, p. 67). It is this condition of reciprocity that distinguishes the

I-You relation, as manifested in the human-to-human encounter, from the encounter with the "It" world. As Buber (1970) goes on to explain,

> In the It-world causality holds unlimited sway. Every event that is either perceivable by the senses and "physical" or discovered or found in introspection and "psychological" is considered to be of necessity caused and a cause .... The unlimited sway of causality in the It-world, which is of fundamental importance for the scientific ordering of nature, is not felt to be oppressive for the man [or woman] who is not confined to the It-world but free to step out of it again and again into the world of relation. Here I and You confront each other freely in a reciprocity that is not involved in or tainted by any causality; here man finds guaranteed the freedom of his being and of being. (p. 100)

And here also, amidst this freedom, grounded in respect and reciprocity, is the dimension of responsibility. Following Buber, therefore, the challenge is to adopt a relational research ethics that preserves and honors the difference about which he speaks and does so in a way that underscores this dimension of responsibility.

***

It is precisely at this juncture that the seminal work of Emmanuel Levinas becomes most relevant. "(T)here arises, awakened before the face of the other, a responsibility for the other to whom I was committed before any committing, before being present to myself or coming back to self" (1999a, pp. 30–31). As Levinas quickly goes on to ask,

> What does this *before* mean? Is it the before of an *a priori*? But would it not in that case come down to the priority of an idea that in the "deep past" of innateness was already a present correlative to the *I think*, and that—retained, conserved, or resuscitated in the duration of time, in temporality taken as the flow of instants—would be, by memory, re-presented? (p. 31)

In other words: Is my responsibility—in this case, my responsibility to the other person or persons with whom I am engaged in the research situation—a function of some idea or principle that is now being recollected and enacted in my encounter?

Levinas's answer is a firm No: "Here I am, in that responsibility cast back toward something that was never my fault, never my doing, toward

23

something that was never in my power, nor my freedom—toward something that does not come back to me from memory." For Levinas, therefore, my "responsibility for the other is not reducible to a thought going back to an idea given in the past to the 'I think' and rediscovered by it" (1999a, p. 32). On the contrary, this responsibility is called forth, primordially, by the very "face" of the other person.

> Indeed, it is not a question of receiving an order by first perceiving it and then obeying it in a decision, an act of the will. The subjection to obedience precedes, in this proximity to the face, the hearing of the order. Obedience preceding the hearing of the order—which gauges or attests to an extreme urgency of the commandment, in which the exigencies of deduction that could be raised by an "I think" taking cognizance of an order are forever adjourned. An urgency by which the imperative is, "dropping all other business." (pp. 33–34)

These are difficult words. Some of them—for instance, "obedience," "order," "commandment"—seem downright excessive, hyperbolic. Levinas himself recognizes this: "'Subjection to an obedience preceding the hearing of the order'—is this just insanity and an absurd anachronism?" (p. 34). Some readers may be asking the same question. What relevance can these elaborate words have for theorizing relational research ethics?

As important as Buber's notion of the "between" may be for establishing a properly dialogical view of relational research ethics, Levinas seeks to move beyond it, precisely by positing what I earlier referred to as "the priority of the Other" (Freeman, 2014a). As he explains, drawing on some of Buber's own language,

> The I-Thou relation consists in placing oneself before an outside being, i.e. one who is radically other, and in recognizing that being as such. This recognition of alterity does not consist in forming an idea of alterity. Having an idea of something belongs to the realm of I-It. It is not a question of thinking the other person, or of thinking him or her as other—but of addressing that person as a Thou. The adequate access to the alterity of the other is not a perception, but this saying of Thou. There is immediate contact in this invocation, without there being an object … The I-Thou relation, then, appears from the outset to escape the gravitational field of the I-It in which the alleged exteriority of the object remains held. (Levinas, 1996a, p. 22)

So far, so good; Buber and Levinas appear to be of a piece. But Levinas is troubled by certain aspects of Buber's thinking too, particularly the idea of reciprocity. This is "because the moment one is generous in hopes of reciprocity, that relation no longer involves generosity but the commercial relation, the exchange of good behavior …. [T]he other appears to me as one to whom I owe something, toward whom I have a responsibility" (1999a, p. 101). Levinas (1996a) therefore asks:

> How can we maintain the specificity of the interhuman I-Thou without bringing out the strictly ethical meaning of responsibility, and how can we bring out the ethical meaning without questioning the reciprocity on which Buber always insists? Doesn't the ethical begin when the I perceives the Thou as higher than itself? (p. 32)

Levinas (1996b) elaborates on this idea of height when he writes:

> The putting into question of the self is precisely a welcome to the absolutely other. The other does not show itself to the I as a theme. The epiphany of the Absolutely Other is a face by which the Other challenges and commands me through his nakedness, through his destitution. He challenges me from his humility and from his height … The I is not simply conscious of this necessity to respond, as if it were a matter of an obligation or a duty about which a decision could be made; rather the I is, by its very position, responsibility through and through. And the structure of this responsibility will show how the Other, in the face, challenges us from the greatest depth and highest height—by opening the very dimension of elevation. (p. 17)

There is more. "The one for whom I am responsible is also the one to whom I have to respond. The 'for whom …' and the 'to whom …' coincide. It is this double movement of responsibility which designates the dimension of height" (p. 19).

As opposed to Buber, therefore—or at least Levinas's rendition of Buber—"There would be an inequality, a dissymmetry, in the Relation, contrary to the 'reciprocity' upon which Buber insists, no doubt in error" (1999b, p. 150). Levinas thus wants to go beyond Buber's dialogical form of relationality, his assumption being that it embodies an implicit contractuality, a mutual indebtedness that cannot help but detract from the purity of the for-the-Other relation. However important Buber's dialogical perspective may be in underscoring the primacy of the relational, it stops short of being truly ethical for Levinas, for the ethical, in his view, is precisely about the priority—the height—of the Other, and it is this priority that bespeaks the dissymmetry of the ethical relation. As for the idea of responsibility, it is, again, not to be understood as "a cold juridical exigency," in the sense of a thematizable idea or principle that one applies to the situation in question. Rather, "It is all the gravity of the love of the neighbor" (p. 163), the responsibility I have, the responsibility I *am*, "coming from before my freedom, from before all beginnings in me, and from before every present" (p. 166). Levinas is speaking here of a primordial responsibility, one that precedes the decisions one makes, the duties one needs to fulfill, or the particular responsibilities one has. The priority of the Other thus entails the primacy not just of the relational but of the ethical; responsibility, to and for the Other, is its mandate.

Seen from one angle, it may seem that Levinas's perspective cannot readily be applied to the research situation—if, by research situation, we are referring to the kind of situation one enters armed with a particular research agenda. If, in fact, I am interested in learning something about this or that phenomenon, via becoming engaged with this or that person or group of persons, how can I possibly avoid directing the course of the encounter, however gently, however unobtrusively? If "the ethical begins when the I perceives the Thou as higher than itself," isn't my research agenda compromised from the start? Strictly speaking, it may very well be. However generous, empathic, and relationally minded a researcher may be, there is a very basic sense, again, in which he or she aims to "get" something from his or her research participants. Indeed, it might even be argued that the research relationship is, on some level, inevitably an I-It relationship. How can one establish a truly relational research ethics given this most basic arrangement? Is it even possible? And to return to the more pointed question I posed at the outset of this chapter: How might I justify this particular project? Can I?

I could argue that writing about my mother meets some elements of the "social justice" framework discussed by Josselson, insofar as it may "lead to empowerment of the participants and/or the group they represent and also engender better societal treatment of those whom they study." I could also argue that it meets some elements of the "basic science" framework she discusses, which posits that "greater knowledge of human experience will lead to a more humane society." Following Buber and especially Levinas, finally, I could argue this writing meets elements of what might be called a "compassion and responsibility" framework, or some other such Other-directed conception. Following Levinas (1999a), this sort of framework should be understood as preceding matters of social justice, coming before them, serving as the primordial, ethical ground upon which they emerge.

Relational research, Levinasian style, might thus be seen as oriented primarily toward the ethical relation itself. Are any of these defenses sufficient to warrant and justify my efforts? I don't have clean answers to any of these questions. The issues at hand may best be left in question form in any case.

***

Now that I have provided some context for the kind of research projects in which I have been and continue to be engaged, I want to take a closer look at the relational dimension as it emerged in the context of my relationship with my mother. The task is an awkward one. As I have already said, I never approached my mother as a researcher. I never arrived at her place with any research agenda. I never had any specific questions in mind. Nor, more generally, did I ever hope to "get" anything from her; whatever I "got," by way of profound words, meaningful actions, and so on, emerged organically in the course of our relationship, through the many hours per week I spent with her. In what follows, therefore, I won't be addressing how the research relationship evolved, but will instead focus on our interpersonal relationship itself, how it moved, by degrees, from being one in which I had my own *personal* agenda—my own images of how she ought to be responding to her situation, my own attempts to direct the course of things, my own "corrections" of her "misguided" view of her very life, and so on—to one in which she was the true priority and I, in turn, her "hostage" (Levinas, 1996c).

This idea of being a hostage may seem odd, even impertinent, but it came to be an important idea in Levinas's thinking. What does he mean, and how might it apply in the present context? In his essay "Substitution" (1996c), he spends some time addressing the curious state of the ego: "The ego is not merely a being endowed with certain so-called moral qualities, qualities which it would bear as attributes," but instead is always in the process "of being emptied of its being, of being turned inside out." Moreover, "The ego is not a being which is capable of expiating for others; it is this original expiation which is involuntary because prior to the initiative of the will" (p. 86). In keeping with Levinas's idea of responsibility as being beyond thematization, beyond some principle that I might apply to this or that situation, we see here its "involuntary" nature. And it is precisely this involuntary dimension—our "captivation," one might say, by the Other—that leads him to the metaphor of the hostage: "It is through the condition of being a hostage that there can be pity, compassion, pardon, and proximity in the world—even the little there is, even the simple 'after you sir'" (p. 91). Or in the case of my relationship with my mother, even the simple, "Hey, Ma. Want to go outside and sit in the sun for a while, feel the warm breeze, maybe have a sweet snack?" I will do whatever you want, whatever you need. Period.

> My responsibility in spite of myself—which is the way the other's charge falls upon me or disturbs me, that is, is close to me—is the hearing or understanding of this cry. It is awakening. The proximity of a neighbor is my responsibility for him; to approach is to be one's brother's keeper; to be one's brother's keeper is to be his hostage. Immediacy is this. Responsibility does not come from fraternity, but fraternity denotes responsibility for the other, antecedent to my freedom. (Levinas, 1996d, p. 143)

Even if responsibility does not derive from fraternity—or in the present case, the condition of being a son—it is, arguably, intensified by it. The notion that we are as responsible to the stranger as we are to the family member or friend stands, as ethics. But the situation changes on the psychological plane. I may have been a hostage to everyone on the floor where my mother would eventually live. I heard all of their cries. But not in the same way I heard hers.

It would take some time before I could give myself over to my mother in this way. Even then, this giving-over was, and could only be, partial—aspirational, one might say—owing to the seemingly inevitable intrusion of my own ego-driven needs and wishes, issuing their own demands. From this perspective, and as I shall show in greater detail shortly, affirming the priority of the Other, in the research relationship and elsewhere, is never wholly unalloyed, ego-free, "pure." Indeed, however primordial the ethical relation may be, it can be and frequently is overwhelmed by what Iris Murdoch (1970), following Freud in broad outline, refers to as the "fat relentless ego" (p. 51). This is no doubt one reason why human relations are as fraught as they are. It's also by way of reiterating that I have no interest in portraying myself as some sort of caregiver-hero. There were times when I thought about going over to see Mom and didn't. In addition, and again, there were times when my own preoccupations took center stage, with the result that she became veiled, her face all but occluded from view. I also avow that there were some quite mundane, even egocentric, reasons for my going to see her. As I put the matter elsewhere (Freeman, 2014a), "I go to see her because that's what you're supposed to do, or so she knows what a good son I am, or to assuage some of my own guilt." "But," I continued,

> I also go to see her for her—because she is alone and in need and my visit brings her one of her few moments of pleasure in life. It's not

easy. I often dread going up in the elevator to her floor; there is always something disturbing or depressing going on. Leaving is no better. I go marching off to work or dinner while she sits in a circle with fading, withered, like-minded others, watching some awful TV show or tapping a balloon into the air during "recreation" period. But in the middle is … her, her simple presence, disrupting me, drawing me forward, outward. She is sitting in a wheelchair, slouched, eyes closed. I walk over and tap her lightly on her shoulder or fiddle playfully with her hair. Her eyes crawl open, she turns her head toward me, and she smiles a faint but radiant smile. I so want her to feel whatever joy she can. (p. 20)

I am not proposing that relationally oriented researchers ought to tap the shoulders of their research participants or play with their hair. Nor am I suggesting that they should have as their primary goal bringing joy to those whose lives they are exploring. The situation I have been addressing is not a typical research situation, and the sort of unfettered "availability" I have just described may seem utterly impertinent in other contexts. Nevertheless, the idea of letting the person or persons in question direct the course of the inquiry and drawing the resultant data from the ongoing movement of relationship itself, wherever it may go, strikes me as a potentially valuable counterweight to the more acquisitive, agenda-driven style of most social science research. In some respects, this approach is a phenomenological one, rooted in what I earlier referred to as practicing fidelity to the lived reality of the lives being explored. It is also a devotional one, one might say, in which giving oneself over to the other and prioritizing her life and well-being is key.

In the end, I came to see the relationship I established with my mother, and the more general idea of approaching another person emptied of self-interest and giving oneself over to her in care as a kind of ideal type—which is to say, a form of human relatedness that bears within it the kind of being held hostage by the Other that Levinas describes. He has been criticized for being hyperbolic in framing human relatedness in this way. I am open to a similar criticism in the way I have framed relational research ethics. What can it possibly mean to give oneself over to the other person in the context of the kind of research most people do? What exactly is being called for here? How is it to be brought into practice? There are no simple answers to these questions. What may be most important, in any case, is the kind of ethical attitude one adopts as one carries out research. For Josselson, you will recall, such an attitude "involves deep contemplation about what it means to encounter and represent 'otherness'" and "mandates that the researcher question personal assumptions about the normal, healthy, or desirable" (p. 555). It also mandates that one try to meet others where they are, no matter where they are, and to do so without judgment, expectations, needs, or wishes—without *will*, in a way. This may ultimately be impossible. But holding such an attitude in mind as a kind of regulative idea and ideal may nevertheless be of value in carrying out relational research, as well as living out the kind of human relations to which we may aspire.

The perspective being advanced herein may well strike some readers as too radical, too far removed from the norms and necessities of social science research, however sensitively it may be carried out. One reason, discussed earlier, is that the very idea of a research agenda is inevitably undercut, even undermined, by the kind of relational stance being suggested: Insofar as the Other is given priority, I—my wishes and needs, my goals and objectives as a researcher—am relegated to a distinctly "secondary" position. Ultimately, I had to go where my mother led me. For me to have done anything else would have been patently unethical; it would have meant controlling her in some way, directing the course of action in such a way as to produce a result, a "finding." This situation was of course unique in some ways; as such, I am not in a position to recommend such an "aimless" relational stance to others. Nevertheless, this aimlessness, this stance of being-led-by rather than leading, stands as a regulative ethical idea and ideal.

The other reason the perspective being advanced may be deemed too radical or impracticable is that upholding the priority of the Other in the research relation also means serving the person or persons in question—not just acting on their behalf, in the sense of meeting some particular need or serving some social justice cause, but *being* on their behalf. This stance is in keeping with Levinas's (1985) positing of "responsibility as the essential, primary and fundamental structure of subjectivity" (p. 95). Can researchers really be expected to adhere to such a stance? Can one truly approach the research situation in such a way that the ethical comes first, that the person or persons in question not only "lead the way," as above, but direct the very meaning and purpose of one's engagement? Strictly speaking, probably not; the project of research itself would seem to militate against it. But just as the aforementioned aimlessness may be seen as a regulative idea and ideal, so too may the ethical priority of the Other. Moving in this direction leads to a very different conception of the research endeavor. Difficult though it may be to put fully into practice, it may nonetheless be worth considering, at least by those of us seeking to reimagine and perhaps reconstruct the research relationship.

CHAPTER 2

PROTEST

I can't remember many of the details that led me to bring my mother to the Department of Neurology at the University of Massachusetts (UMass) Medical Center in Worcester, where my family and I have lived for 30-plus years. By June 2003, I knew something was amiss. She was having memory lapses, mainly in the form of repeat stories and the like. She was also just "off" in her ability to perform some of the basic activities of daily living, and she was beginning to do some weird things, like putting her purse in the oven. This was supposedly for the sake of safekeeping, and it may have been. When I asked her about why she had left the purse there, she told me that it was something of a family tradition, that others had done it too. Okay, if you say so. But she had never done this before, and antics like this told me that a change was in the making. I wanted to find out what was going on.

My mother didn't have much of a sense that she was entering a new phase, or at least she acted as if she didn't. Sure, her memory wasn't quite what it had once been, but isn't that just what happens with older people? Sometimes I wondered if she was right about this. After all, despite some worrisome memory slips, confusion over bills, and my concerns about her being off in some way, she continued to live much the same life she'd been living. At what point is a concerned son supposed to look into these changes anyway?

A hospital stay in Florida, where she had been living for half the year (the other half in Worcester), proved to be something of a tipping point. It was difficult to know what was going on down there. Her accounts of things were muddled and confused, and it was only by speaking directly with doctors and nurses that we could gather a clear picture.

Aside from this difficult hospital stay, it was mainly her repetition—of utterances, stories, questions, and so on—that led us to make an appointment with a neurologist at UMass. My mother took care of some of the details herself by contacting the hospital in Florida where she had stayed.

I respectfully request that you please forward at once the complete records of my stay—tests, results, medications, treatments, X-rays, doctors' notes—EVERYTHING—to [her neurologist].

Please, please send post haste ~ I thank you in advance!

Post haste! Ever the wordsmith, my mother was. She had been great at completing *The New York Times* crossword puzzles. She was also a terrific Scrabble player. She had never been to college; she instead attended a local business school for a spell, to sharpen some of her bookkeeping and clerical skills. She was hardly a card-carrying "intellectual," but she was smart and quick and very knowledgeable about lots of things. Even when she was far along in her dementia, I could ask her what a word meant or how to spell it, and for the most part, she would be right there. She retained amazing long-term memory too, at least for some things. In the later years of her nursing home stint, she had only the vaguest memory of my father. The same was true with Rocky, the man she had spent 15 happy years with following my father's death in 1975.

Eventually, there would be virtually nothing. But even then, late in the game though it was memory-wise, she was always the runaway winner whenever there were trivia contests. When it came to playing Name That Tune or singing along with the visiting one- or two-man bands there to play the old favorites, she would be the lead voice for those too. It was shocking in a way. There she'd be, huddled in a wheelchair, eyes shut, seemingly oblivious to the world, just *being*, another broken person in what often appeared to be a kind of benign stupor. Until the contests and activities began. Well, look at that. Marian's awake after all!

I have to say, I think she was the favorite resident on her floor. For one, she generally remained polite and courteous to the many people who tended to her. For another, she could be surprisingly lively at times, emerging from her apparent slumber to call out a trivia answer or to utter a caustic wisecrack when one of her fifth-floor cronies got out of hand. "We don't need *that!*" she once said in response to one of her screaming floormates. Another time, when a man nearby was doing a combination of yelling, moaning, and singing, I asked, "Does it bother you? Do you find it weird?"

"Yes," she said, "he's a weirdo. But that's *his* problem, not mine!"

***

I didn't expect to write the words you've just read. I had intended to tell the story at hand by beginning at the beginning, the day I took her to see the neurologist. But there was something about those words, "post haste," that called forth other memories, other kinds of memories, more spirited and celebratory. Did I turn to those as a way of avoiding, if only temporarily, the pain of our visit to the neurologist?

For those of you who elected to skip over the previous chapter in order to get to the story, I noted that this inaugural visit to the neurologist was indeed a painful one. I won't pretend to have a clear memory of it. I know that the doctor did what he could to discern and diagnose my mother's situation. This meant speaking with her about her life, giving her a "mini-mental" (a diagnostic test designed to gauge one's level of cognitive functioning), and having her undergo magnetic resonance imaging (MRI), which would allow him to see what might be going on, or not going on, in her brain. She did fairly well on the mini-mental, though her performance did indicate some "mild cognitive impairment." *Mild.* All things considered, that doesn't sound too bad, does it? In some ways, this relatively benign label simply concretized what we already knew. Yes, there was some cognitive impairment; that's why we made the appointment. What about the MRI? Would we learn anything new from that? Well, yes; there was some excess "white stuff" lurking in her brain, and this suggested that mild though her impairment was at the moment, it was likely a function of Alzheimer's disease. We therefore knew were at the beginning of what would no doubt be a long, arduous haul.

My mother had always been terribly fearful of Alzheimer's. One of her aunts, a lovely woman whom everyone adored, had fallen victim to the disease and had become a shell of who she had been. Then there was one of her friends, energetic and vivacious, who, in relatively short order, had come equally undone. So it came as no great surprise that when the neurologist uttered those two dreaded words—Alzheimer's disease—my mother would sink, low. She was too polite and modest in her ways to break down in the neurologist's office. But I know that she was hurting, badly.

Okay, then. Okay. Thank you. See you again sometime soon.

And then she wept, a deep and despairing flood of tears, of a sort I'd never seen before. Well, maybe once, when my dad died, but that was a long time ago, nearly 30 years, and this was fresh and real and terrible. Her very future. Her very *fate.* It's so hard to see a parent, a mother, suffer. So, so hard.

I'm feeling it right now. It's been a while since I wept for her, possibly because I put off writing about her for a while. I had intended to. But something had stopped me. I just couldn't do it, or at least I couldn't do it in the way I knew I had to. I guess the good news is that I'm doing it that way now. My tears, and the lump in my throat, and the numbness coursing through my body and my soul are proof.

***

It was especially hard for me to see my mother suffer. She and I had always been extra close. When my dad died in 1975, both of my brothers were already married with kids; one is eight years old than me, the other six. I was still in college, ready to start my junior year, 20 years old and still pretty close to the nest. So when my brothers eventually went home to their families, I stayed home with Mom, doing what I could to help her navigate this new, awful situation.

I don't mean to suggest that I suddenly became some sort of homebound servant to my mother; I had my own life to live and I liked to have a good time. Devoted to my mother though I was, or at least aspired to be, I hardly became a virtuous shut-in. Nor do I mean to elevate myself above my brothers; our situations were very different. But the fact is, my mother and I spent a lot of time together back then, laughing, crying, screaming at one another for the latest infraction, and more. It was the classic best of times, worst of times. I don't recall all of my moves, but I know I performed some serious psychological gymnastics during those years. Wanting to be by her side but distancing myself from her. Channeling my guilt and shame into rage and indignation. I fled a couple of times—first on a two-month jaunt across Canada a year after my dad's death; then a few months cruising around Europe; later, a nine-month, cross-country trek with a couple of old buddies. Looking back, I find it surprising that I left my mother alone as much as I did. Some of it was probably just restlessness, wanting to explore the world, do my thing. But I also wonder whether I needed to make sure I wasn't too tethered to her.

Through it all, though, we were close. One time, we took a trip together to St. Martin, where one of her cousins had a funky little apartment on the French side. We always enjoyed knocking down some gin and tonics at day's end and chatting about this or that. We would confide in one another too; I remember one time in particular, some eight years after my dad's death, when Mom broke down and moaned, "I thought it was supposed to get easier." Difficult to hear. Had she been suffering the entire time? On the face of it, things had changed substantially: She had moved from our old house into an apartment in a quaint, village-style town about ten miles away. She had re-entered the work world after some 32 years as a homemaker. And she had become tough—or at least tougher than she had been—in a kind of on-edge, New York way, ever on the lookout for being cheated or messed with. Some of this was no doubt a defense against her inner vulnerability and her lingering feeling that she had been robbed, of her precious husband and of the life they had planned. Gone, forever. Or so it seemed.

Things took a decided turn for the better when she started seeing Rocky—Rocco Casella—who had been a member of the Friday night dance group my mother and father were part of, and who had lost his wife around the same time I lost my dad. He was a very different character than my father: an Italian don with a thick New York accent, a former boxer with a great big Cadillac who attended church every Saturday and enjoyed bountiful feasts, home and elsewhere, where he and my mother would consume, and when warranted (and sometimes when not), criticize. They weren't particularly sophisticated, but they both fancied themselves connoisseurs who knew, or believed they knew, how things were supposed to be. Rough-hewn mavens. Rocky was a prince, though, who loved my mother and catered to her in every way he could, even though she had made it clear, repeatedly, that despite his deep desire to marry her (and despite the fact that they sometimes shacked up for months at a time), they would never tie the knot and make it official. I never entirely understood why she refused, but I think it had something to do with her fear that she might lose another husband. Better to keep it informal. That way, if he dies, it won't be quite the same kind of loss as the one she had already suffered.

And die he did, of cancer, after 15 years with my mother. I remember hearing the news. It was the day I turned 40, and he had told my mother that I was to go out and get a great bottle of wine, a passion we all shared. I got a terrific Beringer cabernet and dug into it that very night, just as he would have wanted. There would be more such indulgences at the bountiful Italian feast that followed his funeral.

Appearances aside, Rocky and my dad were alike in some ways too, especially in their great love of good food and drink. My dad was a Jewish kid from Boston with a very different style—Chevrolets, not Cadillacs. But he too was a tough guy of sorts, with a hard shell and a sweet interior, and he too was madly in love with my mother, fiercely dedicated to her, and even when his occasional "black moods" hit, she was never the target of his despair or rage. I'm sure they had their occasional fallings-out; I can remember one very distinctly. For some inconceivable reason, Dad bought Mom a broiler for their anniversary one year. Not a good idea. Back it went. And back he went, to find something a bit more suited to the occasion. She was hardly an ardent feminist, but Mom had some spunk, I must say.

Rocky's death hurt too, but in a different way. My mother grieved, to be sure, but she didn't sink into despondency as she had before. Among other reasons, she had family close by when she lost Rocky, both in Florida and in Worcester, so she wasn't as intensely lonely as she had been. Plus, she hadn't lost the "love of her life" this time around. As the phrase suggests, that was a one-time affair, and whether she didn't love Rocky as much or couldn't or wouldn't, the wound wasn't nearly as deep.

***

Outside of some physical complications that came her way now and then, the next eight or so years passed uneventfully. My brothers and I went on a cruise with our families to celebrate Mom's 75th birthday. A few years later, she came to visit our family when we lived in Spain for the year. We celebrated that birthday in Madrid, at Sobrino de Botín, allegedly the oldest restaurant in the world, around since 1725, best known for its amazing *cochinillo*, suckling pig. (Good Jews!) From there, we all drove down to our apartment in Seville and showed her the sights. She was so vibrant and alive—and stylish. My wife still wears the red leather jacket that Mom bought in Seville. Pretty cool. There was another big family gathering in the Catskills when she turned 80, where we all gorged ourselves on uninspired but scarily abundant food and sat at our tables listening to Borscht Belt comedians riff on suburban New York culture. It's hard to believe that a mere six months later, in the summer of 2003, she would receive that dreadful diagnosis.

***

What should we make of the diagnosis anyway? The doctor did utter the word "Alzheimer's." But wasn't it the case that you really don't know for sure until a postmortem examination? That was essentially what I said in response to a note from my sister-in-law, who appeared to be more certain of the diagnosis than I was. "I hope you don't find this a patent act of denial on my part," I wrote to her,

> but I'm not sure I'd say the neurologist was "as certain as could be" about the Alzheimer's diagnosis. She likely does have Alzheimer's; her symptoms are unquestionably consistent with it. But the neurologist himself was actually somewhat vague in how he spoke about things. Initially, he spoke

mainly in descriptive fashion about "mild cognitive impairment." Only when we probed a bit did he move into Alzheimer's territory.

I'm not trying to do a denial thing here (I don't think). It's as plain as day that something is amiss, and getting more so. Like you, I'm doing some "reading up" ... Right now, though, I'm not entirely sure how far to go with the Alzheimer's label—which, as I understand it, has become something of a catch-all diagnosis for many forms of cognitive decline.

It's difficult to know what to make of my response. There could be an element of denial in it. There was something about that word—*Alzheimer's*—that seemed ominous, resonant with danger and death. It was certainly that way for my mother. Why was it necessary to use that word anyway? What did it add?

My sister-in-law was a trained nurse and was no doubt more comfortable with the word than I was. Part of the trade. For better or worse, I would never utter that word, whether in Mom's presence or elsewhere. When discussing her situation with others or when writing about her, I used the more generic "dementia." It's not a whole lot better; it has its own scary connotations, of madness and loss. But it seemed less scary to me. Whether it would have been less scary to her, I can't say. In my view, there wasn't much reason to use that word either; all it would do, all it could do, was put her in a box. There was no need to go there.

Some years later, when my mother went to spend a few days with my brother and sister-in-law, one of them spoke the word "Alzheimer's" again, I'm not sure in what context, and she broke down once more, awash in a torrent of awful tears. I mention this episode not as a criticism; Ken and Randy are both loving people and had no idea of the consequences of uttering that word in my mother's presence. It's a just a word, after all. Why not be direct about it? Who knows? Maybe there would even be some cathartic effect of facing the reality of it head-on. By all indications, though, the tears my mother shed that day weren't tears of catharsis. Rather, they were tears of shock and horror and grief, for all that had been lost already and for all that inevitably would be lost in the days to come.

Whether I was commendably sensitive to my mother's situation or avoidant or both, I can't say. What I can say is that our fateful visit to the neurologist in the summer of 2003 was brutal, for her most of all, but for me too. I don't know that I formulated it in my mind in exactly this way at the time, but I knew in my heart that it was the beginning of the end, and that in-between the two, there was bound to be immense, crushing suffering. A tragedy was in the making. What else could it possibly be?

***

About a year later, in June 2004, my mother and I met with a social worker who specialized in elder care issues and organizational consulting to take stock of what was going on and to determine how best to move into the future. I am surprised we (I?) waited that long to create a plan. Troubling though her increasingly diminished memory was, her situation wasn't a dire one—not yet. She was still able to carry out basic household functions, my family and I were close by if she needed us, and although she was clearly frustrated at times when faced with tasks that had once been routine, she was determined and able to manage most things independently. There was also a nice pool in her apartment complex in Worcester, and she didn't want to part with that too quickly.

Shortly after our meeting with the social worker, my mother received a report, which I was copied on, that included the following:

> The reason for the meeting was that you have experienced increasing memory problems and are under the care of [your doctor] at the UMass-Memorial Neurology Clinic. After many years of splitting your time between Worcester and Florida, you will now be in Worcester full-time. Your family provides a lot of support but wants to know about additional care options. You recently visited Tatnuck Park assisted living but do not yet feel ready to consider that living option.

> […] You told us that you are not having any difficulties with caring for yourself (bathing, dressing, grooming, eating). You manage the laundry on your own. You do need assistance with housework, cooking, shopping. There may be some problems with financial management, but you and Mark were going to look into ways to simplify your financial life with automatic withdrawals, payments and deposits.

I suppose the report was helpful, but it didn't really tell us anything we didn't already know. Basically, we would have to keep on managing as best we could and make use of whatever resources were available. The social worker, meanwhile, would spread the word to the relevant parties—for instance, a woman at the local Jewish Community Center (JCC) who was responsible for coordinating services for those in need. Fine. In that moment, all we could do was just keep on and begin thinking about what the future would likely bring and how we might address it.

***

Able though my mother remained in many spheres of her life, I had serious concerns about her driving capacities. The neurologist shared these concerns, and suggested that she be tested at a local rehab center that offered an "Adaptive Driving Program." Not surprisingly, Mom was none too happy about this. She was fine! She was always a good driver! Why was this test even necessary? She did finally acquiesce, mainly because the neurologist had recommended it and he carried enough stature and weight for her to comply, however reluctantly. I have to confess, I had hoped she would be deemed sufficiently impaired that her license would be revoked; that way, I wouldn't have to bear the burden of laying down the law. But that's not what happened. Another report:

> Marian Freeman was seen for an on-the-road driving evaluation at Fairlawn Rehabilitation Hospital on June 23, 2004, to assess her ability to safely return to driving. During the evaluation, Ms. Freeman demonstrated good driving habits and skills in a variety of driving environments, including narrow back streets, heavily trafficked urban streets, intersections with differing means of traffic control (stop lights, stop signs, yield signs, etc.), multi-lane roadways and areas with significant pedestrian traffic. The evaluation also including backing-up, making a 3-point turn, making a u-turn and angle parking.

> During the evaluation, I saw no reason why Ms. Freeman should not be able to return to driving independently. Ms. Freeman's performance was consistent over the course of the evaluation, with a minimum number of issues noted.

There was a caveat at the end of the report. As the driving test had taken place along a directed route—as in, turn right here, do a U-turn there—"it is not possible to fully assess Ms. Freeman's memory as it would pertain to route planning and execution. Given the gap in her driving and medical issues, I … recommend that Ms. Freeman limit her driving to familiar areas and at first drive only during low-traffic volume situations."

Great. Not quite flying colors, but not too far off either. Shouldn't I have been happy about her results? Is it possible that I was being over-protective and was seeing more evidence of my mother's diminishment than was actually there? It's possible. But I didn't think so then and I don't think so now.

I'm quite sure the social worker felt the same. About a month after our initial meeting with her, she sent me a note detailing a conversation she'd had with the woman at the JCC, Sue. "She has been calling your mother to participate in events," the note said. "Your mother attended one lunch-out program. Sue found her to be a bit 'in a fog,' but thought she had enjoyed it. Since then, she has declined all invitations stating that she is going out of town, expecting company, has another appointment, etc. It certainly may be that she didn't like the event and doesn't know how to say that or she is overwhelmed with the idea of going out with a group."

Or maybe she found being "looked after" in this way repugnant. *Leave me alone*. Said politely, of course.

***

My mother's situation was unusual in some ways. I don't know if it's right to say that she was skilled at "hiding" her impairment; even when she was significantly impaired in one sphere, she was okay in another. But she certainly *was* skilled in the art of social performance. This was particularly true in the context of phone conversations. Friends or family would sometimes call her after a significant period of time had passed, and be delighted and relieved at how good she sounded. I know that some of them wondered what all the fuss was about. She sounds like she's always sounded! Indeed she often did. It was only when they came to see her, to engage with her, that they realized what was going on. It could be shocking.

Mom also knew what to say when it came time to tell me or Debbie what she had been doing all day. "Oh reading, picking up." Where were all the books, though? She talked a good game, even later on, after she had landed at the Jewish Healthcare Center. "What have you been doing today, Ma?" I would ask. And she'd always have a ready answer. *Busy*. Even when she had been doing nothing at all. She believed it too.

She wasn't always this pleasant. In fact, there were times during the Tatnuck Park years when, upon being asked the same question—"What have you been doing today, Ma?"—she would respond with anger and indignation. "*Nothing*, absolutely nothing!" She had believed that too. But when we asked the aides whether she had participated in any of the activities that had been offered that day, they often said that she had and that she'd enjoyed them. Back then, we sometimes even told her exactly that. Looks like you've been doing some fun stuff after all. Guess it must have slipped your mind!

Silly us. Pointless. And difficult to resist. Or at least it was then.

Which was better: having an activity-filled day and being convinced that she had done nothing, or doing nothing at all and being convinced that she'd been happily busy? It's hard to say. The latter certainly felt better.

***

As for that driving test, it was the caveat that would have to win the day, hopefully with some confirmatory help from her doctor.

Yes, Ma; we know what the results say. Glad you did well.

But no, you're not going to be driving.

You may know how to parallel park, but you may not remember *where* you parked.

You may be okay in familiar territory, but even the familiar is in the process of becoming less so. You can get lost. You can *be* lost. It's just too dangerous, for you and for others.

No.

I didn't like having to play the role of judge and rule-setter. Nor, a few months later, did I like having to take my mother to all the local assisted living places to determine which one might best meet her burgeoning needs. But this had to be done, her neurologist insisted, and it was better to do it sooner rather than later. Why, though? What's the rush? His explanation, terrifying in its way: When the disease advances to a certain point, it can be extremely difficult for a person encountering a new environment to avoid feeling that she has suddenly been thrust into an alien world, unrecognizable, devoid of familiar touchstones. So it was important for her to make the move while she still had some semblance of her wits about her; that way, she would have the time to adjust to her new surroundings and bring them into some measure of familiarity. You don't want to wait on this, the neurologist insisted; things can get distressing and positively chaotic if you do.

We therefore had to visit all of these lovely, scary places, chock-full of old people, many of whom were visibly impaired in some way, even though things were still going tolerably well for my mother herself. What the hell was going on?

We're doing all this based on a prediction about what I'm destined to become?

Don't I have any *say* in this?

Don't I have any say in my own *life*?

What's going on?

***

As Mom had said repeatedly through the years, she never wanted to be burden on any of her kids. Maybe this is what led her, finally, to accept the idea of moving into an assisted living facility. Some of them were pretty nice too: happy hours. Gourmet meals (sort of). Beauty salons. Pools. Bowling alleys! Well, gee, Ma, we're ready to join you! The prospect was jarring, nonetheless—not so much because it was a function of her diagnosis (which she had long forgotten), but because she really didn't seem, or feel, like one of those old people she saw wandering the gardens and the corridors of the places we visited.

It's not surprising that she felt this way. Compared to a lot of those people, she *was* different—more vital, more alive. She was still attractive, and she carried herself in a way that belied her years. The people at Tatnuck Park saw her as different too. When there was a fashion show, Mom was chosen to be the model. When they held their annual holiday gathering, she'd be working the crowd like a pro. She always did like a good party. She danced sometimes too, and others would marvel at her moves and her grace, her ability to still groove. I can't recall the exact event, but once, she was chosen as the belle of the ball or the prom queen or whatever it was, and alongside the king, she danced the night away. There were some good times. But some of these good times were also confusing and disturbing. What *was* she doing there?

Things became that much more confusing and disturbing later on, when she forgot that she had been part of the process of selecting a new place to live and was convinced that my brothers and I had made all the necessary arrangements behind her back.

"I guess none of you wants me," she said one time.

Ugh. It was so hard to resist coming back at her during these times and "reminding" her that she'd been involved in the process.

"You were right there with us, Ma!"

Impossible. Inconceivable. And occasionally, the all-too-familiar refrain: "I think I would remember if I'd been involved!"

Time for me to shut up now, try to distract her in some way, curb her rage.

But that wasn't all. Once she settled into Tatnuck Park, she would sometimes bemoan the fact that none of us ever came to see her, that we had abandoned her, left her all alone.

"That's not true!" I often exclaimed pathetically. "Debbie and I come to see you all the time!"

But then came that refrain: "I think I'd remember that," she'd hiss.

But you don't! Don't you get it?

Sometimes I couldn't help myself and said something like: Of all the people you think abandoned you, you're telling this to *me*?! Seriously? Your dutiful son who's gone to the mat for you?!

Just stop, Mark. She can't do otherwise. She has dementia, for Chrissake! You *know* that. So get over yourself, with your anger and your hurt feelings.

Got it. Will do. When I can.

It would take a while.

***

It was late fall 2004, and my mother had just moved into Tatnuck Park. She complained, sometimes vehemently, about living there—and about my brothers and I having put her there. Reasons abound.

Foremost among them was the fact that she often had no idea at all why she was there, and she resented it immensely. Many of the people there annoyed her. A new woman moved in, and apparently, every time she finished with dinner, she asked my mother where the Bingo game was being played.

"She asks the same question over and over again!" my mother said angrily. "She's stupid!"

"It's got nothing to do with stupidity," I told her. "It sounds like she's got some memory problems, and if truth be known," I added, as gently as possible, "they're similar to yours."

My mother is momentarily speechless, both knowing and not-knowing at the same time. And then a couple of minutes later she tells the same story yet again, displaying through her own repetition the exact same malady she has just condemned.

I too am speechless.

***

Then there was the conversation I had with Mom about some family plans. She had left me a panicky telephone message about people coming to visit her, but was confused about the details and needed to speak with me. "I think Lissy (her daughter-in-law) is picking me up tonight to take me to the Cape," she said. I told her that I seriously doubted that; having spoken to Lissy just the night before, I knew that she had plans to take my mother to the Cape two weeks later. A day earlier, she had been convinced that her sister was coming to visit the following day, and that my brother, Ken, and his wife were visiting a week from then.

"No," I had told her, "I am quite sure Ken is coming to your place tomorrow." Did that mean that she was having multiple visitors tomorrow? "Call your sister," I said, "and see when she's coming, this week or next. Then call me so I know who's coming when." Her sister was in fact coming the following week. So, Ken was visiting tomorrow, her sister next week. Fine. But just after things had settled down, she received a call from Lissy. Mom came undone.

It was information overload. Everything was getting jumbled together; the visitors were the same and the dates of visit were the same, but they had become severed from one another. So when she woke up the next morning and tried to piece together this confusing puzzle, panic set in. At this point, I simply tried to calm her down and reassure her that only one person, Ken, was coming to visit that weekend. Her sister was coming the following weekend, and Lissy, the one after that. Just to make sure, I promised her I would call Lissy. Yes, she was planning to visit in two weeks. So I called my mother back right away to confirm the situation. She broke down, distraught over the very being she had become.

"Oh, Mark, *what am I going to do*? Sometimes you just live too long …."

***

My mother was living in a kind of liminal psychic space. Despite her occasional recognition of her difficulties, she would either downplay them (she had actually spoken lightheartedly of having "CRS" [Can't Remember Shit] syndrome), or remain vehement about her abilities. "I know I can still drive just fine," she would say. "I've always taken care of my own papers." "I've never been late with a check."

I sometimes questioned these abilities. "Ma, there's a chance you'll get lost when you're driving." "Your papers are in a state of chaos." "Actually, you *have* been late with several checks."

Her response was often swift and to the point: "You're treating me like a child." Or, "I'm not an imbecile." I sometimes found myself trying to explain that things were different now, that some of the things she used to be able to do, very competently, she could no longer do.

"I want to get some kind of job," she announced once, maybe office work of the sort she had done years ago.

"That really may not be the best job for you at this point," I told her. "There are some things you can do just fine, but other things are harder for

44

you now." Generally speaking, however, it didn't sink in. It was difficult to determine whether this was a function of incomprehension or denial or both.

It wasn't clear to me how to address these momentary confusions and shocks. Should I level with her, tell her exactly what's been going on? Cushion it in some way? Fib? Redirect?

I was more committed to telling her the truth in the early years than I was in the later ones. I would try to do it gently and with compassion, but there was a part of me that wanted her to know. I still think that was the right thing to do, at least at the time. And yet I'm not entirely sure how many of my "I hate to break this to you, Ma" moments were for her sake and how much they were for mine.

***

As nice as it was, the very nature and ambience of Tatnuck Park made things that much more fraught. "Bus trips to get ice cream!" "Bingo every night!" "Everybody goes upstairs to bed at eight o'clock!" Many of my mother's peers had walkers or wheelchairs and looked very old and fragile. She didn't look like them at all; she was youthful and moved briskly, still confident in her step. Consequently, these people and the activities they pursued sometimes annoyed and upset her. We therefore found ourselves looking for ways to help her, unsure whether "adjustment" was the answer or something else.

"What do you *want*?" I asked her one time.

Her answer: "*I want to be a person.*"

That was a gut punch. My brothers and I meant well, and this was no time for second-guessing. But what had been done—what *we* had done, her own "consent" notwithstanding—had apparently deprived her of her very sense of personhood.

When she had lived alone, my mother went on to say, she had been a "free agent," able to walk over to the local drugstore, to come and go as she pleased. And she could drive. Now, though, there was only that rickety old Tatnuck Park van. And there were all those old people. To paraphrase her, it was all just nothingness, an endless cycle of meals and activities and outings. How had it come to this?

***

There was an image still in view of a full and whole person, independent, free, of sound mind and body. There is a story that could be told about this

45

person. It is the story of a child whose parents were too poor to keep her and who sent her off to a children's home for a couple of years, a home she had quite loved. It's the story of a teenager, a bit shy but the smartest in the class; of a young woman, competent and hardworking, going it alone while her husband was away in India during the war; of a middle-aged woman, prematurely widowed, who, after years of being a homemaker, had to go out into the work world once more, where she excelled, rising to the position of office manager, in charge of lots of people and able to make the whole outfit run smoothly and efficiently. This story still seemed to be with my mother. How dare anyone suggest that she could no longer balance a checkbook. She had balanced books for a living, and she was damn good at it! On one level, the continued presence of this story was surely a good thing. But it was also the source of much of her frustration and sorrow.

At this stage, there was a severe disjunction between what my mother was and what she was in the process of becoming: a "once-able but no-longer" person. And she knew it. This disjunction no doubt exists for many aging people, maybe even all to some degree. I've been feeling it this week. I was once able to climb significant hills on my bicycle with ease. Now, it seems, I can no longer do it. I was once able to sit and read for long stretches of time. Now, I tend to fall asleep after a little while. It's humbling, even disturbing at times. But not like it was for my mother. For her, it was as if everything was crashing down; all the things that defined her, in her own eyes, were coming undone. *She* was coming undone, and she felt it, acutely. What made the process even more confusing and painful was that she really didn't know why.

She knew she had some problems; the evidence was thrown in her face daily in one way or another. For better and for worse, though, she simply *forgot* many of the things she was no longer able to do. She had minimal memory of her lost purse or checkbook (or whatever), and if we apprised her of these losses, she generally seemed not to believe it. Not unlike many others with dementia, she often convinced herself that these things must have been taken from her, perhaps stolen. It could not possibly be her own forgetfulness, she insisted; it had to be someone else. She believed this narrative despite the fact that we eventually managed to locate every single item she had allegedly lost. The same was true of plans we might have made together. One time, for instance, I asked her whether she wanted to visit my brother Ken and his family. It would be a welcome change of scenery, and her great-granddaughter would be there. "Sure," she said. "That sounds wonderful." We even spoke about which weekend she should go. But she forgot all of this, and when she (re)learned that she would soon be leaving to visit my brother and his family, she immediately became convinced that we had orchestrated the entire thing behind her back, as usual, treating her like a child once again. And there was absolutely nothing we could do to convince her of the truth. In time, we stopped even trying.

There were also times when she "remembered" things that *didn't* happen. In the wake of yet another misplaced purse, she told me she had left it at my house when she had been over for dinner. This simply wasn't true. But in her mind, it was, and it remained so. As a result, my wife and I were transformed into the purse-snatchers; it was *our* fault that she didn't have that purse, and we really ought to have taken the time to find it. Here too, there was absolutely nothing that could be said or done to move her from her convictions. At this stage, her ego remained strong and resilient enough to utterly reject the reality before her.

Herein lay her liminal status. Much of the time, she was—subjectively—who she had always been: an office manager and checkbook balancer, able to do just fine, thank you, on her own. ("So buzz off with all your 'help!'") This felt sense of identity was sometimes profoundly interrupted, however, and much to her horror, the story she told herself about who and what she was would suddenly explode. At these times, she found herself living a broken narrative and it was made all the more painful by the felt permanence of the break. There would be no fixing it. The disease was marching forward, inexorably; she was hurtling toward the end. She began having more of these desperate moments. But like so many other things in her life, she often forgot having had them. So she was still looking toward the future, toward the new apartment, the new job, the new *life* that might allow her to recover what had been taken away. Desperate moments were thus frequently replaced by ones that were a curious amalgam of frustration, rage, and hope. I wish these feelings had been distributed more evenly, but there was much more frustration and rage than there was hope. Little wonder that she would frequently protest:

I'm still in control.
I can do it. I still exist.
I'm still a person!
Or at least I want to be.

***

It is precisely at this juncture that cultural reality becomes particularly salient. As suggested earlier, in the background of so much of my mother's frustration and discontent was a highly robust image of who and what she ought to be—manifested in the form of an equally robust, if deluded, image of who she was actually becoming. Back in the Introduction, I spoke of the dual cultural narrative at work in this context. There is "the narrative of the vital, self-sufficient Individual," who vigorously resists feelings of fragility, vulnerability, and dependency. It came as something of a surprise to see just how potent this narrative can be. It is highly resistant to modification too. Consequently, there remained little room for building in a sense of fragility or vulnerability, little room for Mom to admit that things were changing. In part, this was no doubt because of the unconscious dimension of the narrative at hand (Freeman, 2002b, 2010a). It was not something she could look at, hold at a distance. Rather, it was a "master narrative" (Hammack, 2011; Hammack & Toolis, 2015), working through her, permeating her being in ways largely unbeknownst to her.

There is another feature of the narrative of self-sufficiency as well, one that seems extremely pervasive in American culture in particular. In the present case, it had to do with my mother's fervent wish not to be a "burden" on anyone, especially her children. Being unable to drive was so frustrating to her because others, most often my wife or I, had to do it for her. "I hate to rely so much on you," she often said. "I hate to be a burden."

"It's not a big deal," we would say in response. "It's just part of life." But it wasn't part of the life—part of the *narrative* of life—that she was holding onto, however unconsciously, throughout the years. I even tried to deconstruct this narrative with her: "People can rely upon one another," I would say. "Our lives are intertwined. We're not monads but relational beings, and it really is okay that we're doing this with you and for you."

"Thank you, thank you, thank you," she would say when we returned her home, extremely appreciative for the "buggy ride," as she called it. But she very much wished she didn't have to take it. The narrative of self-sufficiency loomed large for her.

This narrative is reinforced by another, which I referred to as "the narrative of inexorable decline." This may culminate in "narrative foreclosure," as I have called it, wherein one effectively becomes convinced that "the story's over" (Freeman, 2000). Old people, with their walkers and their wheelchairs, surrounded my mother. They sat in the lobby, slumped over, dozing, waking briefly when there were passersby. Some of them seemed to have little to do, little left to live for. Their story *was* over, or at least that is how they probably saw it, if they saw it at all. Part of the reason why they saw it this way may be linked to that image of the vital self just considered. They and their like are the inverted image of that self, beyond vitality, beyond self-sufficiency, in some ways, my mother had suggested, beyond personhood itself. She was vehemently *not* them. The nightly Bingo they played downstairs, in open view, really got to her. At the end of the day, there were only mindless games, camaraderie created by random numbers. Time was not to be lived, but simply endured, passed. There was no story to be told after such days; each day was just like the one before and the one before that. My mother sometimes resented these "non-persons" with their non-stories. In her eyes, they had crossed the line, and the image of them sitting there, night after night, was difficult to behold.

My mother wasn't ready to go there. That is, she wasn't ready to join the ranks of these seeming non-persons, and painful though it was, she held fast to what remained of her own personhood, her own autobiographical identity. She still wanted to live a life that was worth telling about, one in which meaningful and significant things happen and could be communicated to other people. This desire brought problems of its own. Sometimes, a trip would be planned—a river cruise, for example. Her hope was that the trip would serve as an Event, a meaningful and significant enough episode to be recounted, gratefully.

"How was the trip, Ma?" We would nervously await her answer. Sometimes, her face was filled with excitement and she would eagerly tell us the story of the day. But more often, it proved to be disappointing.

"We just sat in a boat. We really didn't *do* anything."

And again, the picture could become darker still due to the fact that she may not have remembered much about the trip at all. She often complained about the lack of activities at Tatnuck Park. Maybe she was right, maybe there ought to have been more. As noted earlier, though, we eventually came to realize that many of the activities that did take place—and that she had happily participated in—were quickly forgotten, thereby leading her, again and again, to the conclusion that there was simply nothing to do there.

"But Ma," we would say in response, "you *do* do things there." Materially speaking, this was true. Psychically speaking, however, it was false. And it was her psyche that was leading the way.

***

We had our own forms of protest. They often took the form of correcting her, or trying.

You *do* participate in activities, and you seem to enjoy them too.

You *do* hide your stuff sometimes.

You *forget* all this. Don't you see? *Can't* you see? Why don't you get it?

Our protests became parasitic upon hers. And vice versa, I suppose. We needed to break this chain, this pointless volley back and forth.

***

In a distinct sense, we become the selves we fashion through the imagination. My mother thus became the self that she had imagined through the events, the non-events, and the forgotten events of her life. She complained sometimes about feeling like "nothing." This is no doubt because there was so much "nothing" in the past that she looked back upon daily when we asked her what she did and how it went. In addition to this felt nothingness, there would sometimes be hazy scenes, comprising memories and fantasies and cultural scripts, past, present, and future all interspersed with one another, a veritable mob of meanings. This hazy montage didn't resolve itself very well into a story worth telling, nor did it lead to the kind of self she remembered having been and still wanted to be.

Some of this was likely a function of the biological process of memory loss as it is found in dementia. Short-term memory declines before long-term, and as a result, personal identity is less rooted in the near than in the distant past. This brings us closer to the heart of the existential problem at hand: There remained images, both real and imagined, of the vital, self-sufficient self my mother once was. These images were compelling enough to enter the present. In her own mind, there was a significant part of her that *was* that self, still. At the same time, this vision of the self could not be confirmed or sustained by the day-to-day reality she lived. That reality, bound up as it was with the passing events of the day, was much more transient, much more evanescent. It seemed that there was nothing for her to grab hold of. Or to put it differently, all that could be gotten hold of was: nothing. It was the juxtaposition of these two realities, tied to the distant and near past, the self that was and the self that she had become, that had made things so difficult and had led to so much protest.

***

If truth be told, I sometimes wasn't at my best back then. My mother's incessant repetition of questions could be annoying. Her refusal to believe the truth about all the things that had supposedly been stolen from her was frustrating. And her accusations, especially those having to do with the (alleged) fact that my brothers and I had placed her in assisted living against her will, that none of us wanted her, that Debbie and I never came to see her, and so on, could be downright maddening—this, of course, despite the fact that she was utterly helpless to do anything but exactly what she was doing. So there I was getting angry at my failing, increasingly fragile mother for doing things she couldn't possibly help doing. What a sensitive son!

I sometimes saw myself reacting in the moment and felt ashamed about it. It's as if her situation tapped into a more reactive, primitive side of me. At times, I couldn't help myself, or at least felt I couldn't. It was humbling and disturbing. In addition, it was hard to see her so compromised, and some of my impatience, frustration, and anger were no doubt a function of the fact that, in the end, there was precious little I could do to ease her pain or to halt the inexorable movement of things. It's much easier to see this latter aspect now, looking back, than it was then.

***

If only my mother could have let go, given herself over to her situation and simply lived her life, unhampered by all the cultural scripts and narratives that permeated her existence. I am reminded in this context of Crispin Sartwell's book *End of Story* (2000), which is essentially a diatribe against narrative. Much of our experience, Sartwell reminds us, escapes linguistic articulation. It therefore strikes him as ironic and wrong that so much attention has come to be devoted to narrative as a lens for understanding the human world (see also Strawson, 2004). In addition, and more troublingly, there is the idea that narrative, in its fetish for organization, order, *coherence*, is an oppressive force that we would do well to move beyond. Sartwell even offers a kind of confession early in the book:

> I've tried to live my own life with an extreme degree of coherence; I've tried to understand my own life as a techne, to dedicate it to the realization of well-defined goals. I've tried to rationalize my life: both to live it rationally and to convince myself that I have lived or am living it rationally. I reached a point at which I came to experience the need to do that as a torture. I came to experience the recalcitrance of myself to my will, came to experience the immensity of my own horrible and lovely irrationality. I came also to experience or to admit

the recalcitrance of the world to my will. The latter recalcitrance I could initially narrate as a series of "barriers" to my life-plan. But I reached the point at which I wanted to learn to let the world be instead of trying to transform it into an instrument of my will. (pp. 15–16)

This "torture," and the liberation that followed as Sartwell sought to move beyond narrative in his own life, apparently provided him with a lesson about the underside of narrative itself: It can become a kind of prison, a self-constructed self-enclosure that reduces the bountifulness of experience and subjects it to willful control. There is thus the need for "letting go," for *dis*-ordering one's world. Only then will the "ecstasy" of experience be made possible: "The moment of ecstasy is a moment of vertigo, a vertigo that responds to letting go of one's projects into an all-encompassing present moment" (p. 22).

As Sartwell goes on to argue, drawing especially on philosopher Georges Bataille's *Inner Experience* (1988), narrative is undermined, deconstructed, by the sheer force of certain modes of experience: "Narrative comes apart at the extremes … in ecstasy, in writhing pain, at death" (Sartwell, 2000, p. 65). But that is not all. "[Narrative] has already also come apart everywhere, all the time, wherever people are breathing, or walking around, or watching TV, and not getting anywhere narratively speaking. What narrative is inadequate to is not just the shattering moment, but the moment of indifference" (p. 65). Sartwell even offers us some instruction in this context:

You cannot narrate if you cannot breathe, so shut up for a moment and take a deep breath. Pull yourself away from significance for a moment and let yourself feel the sweet, deep, all-enveloping insignificance all around you. And take comfort in your own insignificance; take comfort in the triviality of your culture; take comfort in the triviality of your life-project and your failure in realizing it. (p. 65)

I'm not sure what Sartwell would have said to my mother given her circumstances, but judging from his words, it might have been something like: Take comfort in the fact that even though you can't drive, or get a job, or maintain your own books, and that consequently you're no longer a Person, you're still alive, well-fed and well-clothed, and able to find meaning in music or joy in your great-grandchild. Sartwell's message is ultimately a quite simple one: *Chill*. Forget about all that "significance" stuff; indifference will undoubtedly leave you a good deal more content with your lot in life. I have been tempted to think like Sartwell myself: *Get over it*; get over your*self*, with your still-kicking projects, your aspirations and fantasies. Those are what are bringing you (and me!) down. But this is precisely what my mother could not do. She was in too deep.

Sartwell can surely identify with this problem. He speaks of feeling the need for meaning as a "pressure, as an anxiety, and furthermore as the project of having some project, and hence as a project that can never be discharged. I live like this," he admits, "busy trying to finish whatever's in front of me as quickly as possible. Then finished. Then feeling empty, subject to attack from my own head. Then inventing or accepting a new project. And so on. I work by projects toward the extinction of project, then can't live there and go on to a new one" (p. 65). So it is that he must tell himself: *Chill*. But it's hard—whether we are narrativists or anti-narrativists, the pressure for meaning, for significance, remains much the same. All he can do, therefore, is try to find some relief. And he does, in caring for his children (who he's "not trying to make … into particular sorts of people"), in playing the accordion or the harmonica (neither of which he's trying to "master"). "Okay," he avows. Playing these instruments is "still trying to do something." So perhaps there's a narrative in there somewhere (the college professor who, much to his chagrin, gets so caught up in trying to defeat discursive thought through discursive thought that's he got to find devices that provide some measure of "surcease from the voice in my head"). "But the point is that the purpose is achieved precisely at the moment that it fades from awareness; those moments are the extinction of project sought by project" (p. 65). He wishes that he "could live there more, that [he] could play more," that there could be "deeper and longer forms of immersion" (p. 66).

I wished this for my mother too. In her case, however, it seemed that there was only one thing that could make this wish come true: the very dissolution of her own autobiographical identity, her own autobiographical *self*—which, of course, would only happen if and when her dementia had run its destructive course. Should we wish for *this*? It would indeed provide her some "surcease" of her own. At the same time, she would also have moved that much closer to oblivion (indifference?) and death. What a strange situation. Was there anything to do in the face of this liminal mode of existence she was living?

* * *

There were three dilemmas—"dilemmas of being," as they might be called—tied to my mother's situation during this initial stage. On the one hand, she was tired and frustrated, at times feeling that her life had gone on long enough. She had no interest in spiraling downward, descending into madness like some of the people she had known through the years; she wanted to avoid that all costs. On the other hand, she remained strenuously committed to pressing on, to being her own person, to keeping herself as connected to the world as possible. This, again, was surely a good thing on some level. But the fact that she had so much difficulty actually doing it—that is, conducting her life in the way that she wished, the way that she once did—made for a very difficult time for all of us. She had thus come to be decidedly ambivalent about nothing less than *being* itself. As I have suggested, one of the deep sources of this ambivalence is the culture in which she lived, with its narratives of self-sufficiency and decline, vitality and loss. She was caught in the middle of these narratives, and at times she couldn't help but feel torn about the very substance of her life.

Occasionally, there were times when it was possible to deconstruct the cultural story in some small way: Maybe it's okay to be vulnerable, to need people, at least once in a while. Maybe the self-sufficiency thing can be taken down a notch. Generally, though, these strategies weren't particularly effective. For one, they require a kind of cultural self-consciousness—an awareness of the ways in which cultural narratives have become constitutive of identity—that my mother didn't have. (There was only so much I could implore her to engage in deconstructive thinking.) For another, her commitment to the narrative of self-sufficiency and her dread of the narrative of decline remained powerful forces in her own ongoing work of being. And work it was—there was hard labor involved in keeping her identity going, with challenges every step along the way. We felt an obligation to help her with this labor, to support her in her ontological work. Deconstructive excursions aside, this meant supporting the narrative of self-sufficiency and helping her maintain independence to the greatest extent possible, even while recognizing that this very support, this very affirmation of autonomy, may have had the unintended and undesired consequence of adding to her frustration and anger.

"Maybe you *can* get a job," I'd say. "There's nothing preventing you from walking to the store. There's plenty, still, for you to do in the world."

I knew how difficult this was for her. She was *not* going to get a job or walk to the store, and concretely speaking, it was no easy task to determine what she could do, at this juncture in her life, that would be as meaningful and significant as she wanted it to be. She simply couldn't do some of the things she wished to do or imagined she could do. This hurt, all around.

The second dilemma of being returns us to some of the frightening territory referred to near the end of the previous section. As committed as we may have been to affirming my mother's autonomy and helping her retain a sense of independence and efficacy, I confess that there were times when we "looked forward" to the future, when a portion of her preoccupation with independence, self-sufficiency, efficacy, *meaning*, would be left behind in the wake of the disease. It's unsettling to think about this issue. Her arrival at this stage would signify a state of profound loss. In all likelihood, she would no longer know who she is, surely not in the sense that she knew herself years ago, and probably not even in the sense that she knew herself in this liminal state we have been considering. Gone would be that sense of rootedness in a history, in *my* history—my past, my story, my identity as *this* person—that characterizes a "normal" self, at least in the modern West. In a distinct sense, *she* would no longer be there, it seemed, and we would need to mourn her loss, even while what remained of that earlier person sat at the dining room table, right across from us, moving in and out of familiarity, recognition. My brothers and I dreaded this future. But she herself would likely suffer less, or at least in a different way, than she was in this liminal state. For also gone would be that backdrop of expectations and images and storylines that were causing so much pain.

Would she ultimately be in a "better place" at that point? It is difficult to say. It all depends on what remains after narrative and the autobiographical self have been left behind. Insofar as she was left with a kind of perpetual nothingness—a state of suspended animation, as it were—it would hardly deserve to be called better, save in the most cursory way. She would have arrived at the land of those "non-persons" she once loathed. The end of narrative would thus spell the beginning of oblivion, of the very *absence* not only of self but also of Other, of world. And even if it is possible that she would be "just fine," subjectively, her frustration and anger having subsided, it is hard to think of this sort of destination as a better place.

This brings me to a final, related dilemma of being, having to do with the very idea of the autobiographical self. More and more, I have come to think of this self as a mixed bag. Some of the reasons have been referred to, both explicitly and implicitly, in this chapter. It can bring pride and pleasure, gratification over one's achievements, and much more. But it can also bring regret and disappointment, shame and frustration, particularly when one's self doesn't measure up to cultural and personal expectations and ideals. Is it possible that the demise of the autobiographical self could yield a state of being that is more than "just fine," in the sense of being largely pain-free, that opens up regions of being that are ordinarily dormant or suppressed? In the Buddhist context especially, there is much talk of moving beyond ego, beyond self. In some quarters, there is also talk of moving beyond narrative. Practices abound for helping people do exactly this. Could dementia, or at least certain forms of it, bring about something similar? These are the kinds of questions I found myself asking toward the end of the first phase of my mother's dementia.

CHAPTER 3

PRESENCE

This chapter will be a good deal briefer than the previous one. This is because the phase being addressed was itself briefer. In fact, I'm not even sure whether to call it a phase, if by that we mean a discrete span of time. What I will be exploring here is more like a possibility, a quite beautiful one, in some ways, that occasionally inserted itself into my mother's life and served as a momentary reprieve from the many burdens that had come her way.

***

My mother always loved music, especially when it was played outdoors, live, on a nice summer evening. So for a time, Debbie and I took her to as many concerts as we could. Mom would be utterly engaged when she was there, totally connected to the music, moving to it like no one else was around. Top it off with a glass or two of wine and some good food and she was where she wanted to be. There were few moments in her life when she was happier, more at peace. Apparently, the story was much the same when she spent some days with her great-granddaughter, Sophie. Pushing the baby in her stroller, up and down a clean suburban street, she had been freed of her burdens, if only temporarily. She had become divested of ego, of self. There was neither a broken narrative nor the stubbornly persistent one that provided so much fuel for her frustration. There was just music, just Sophie. Life had become worthwhile again.

Life would therefore become most worthwhile for her precisely when *she*—qua autobiographical identity—wasn't there. Or to put the matter somewhat differently, if paradoxically, her healthiest and most life-affirming experiences as a self, a vital self, were precisely when her autobiographical identity and narrative were in abeyance. There does remain a self in these instances: the self who loved music (and always had), the self who loved Sophie (and always would). But it is a self that is rooted mainly in the present, in the living moment, in the relation to what is *Other*.

My mother's identity at such moments of unselfconscious attention, immersion, and "flow" (Csikszentmihalyi, 1990) was therefore not so much a *narrative* identity, born out of the particulars of her history, as what might be considered a kind of ontological or spiritual identity, born out of her innermost being, out of those less particularized dimensions of history that had become sedimented in the form of her interests, inclinations, and passions. These were moments of *presence*, that is, of *being present* and indeed being *in* the present, and the very energy and vitality they were able to generate may tell us something important, not only about (I say this cautiously) some potentially positive consequences of dementia—for certain people, at certain times—but also about some of the aforementioned liabilities of the autobiographical self.

My mother's deeply felt experience of music and great-grandchildren, among other things (a beautiful day, a piece of rich, chocolate cake), provided an occasion for what Iris Murdoch (1970) has referred to as "unselfing," a process wherein the otherness of the Other, whatever it may be, displaces ego concerns. "We cease to be," she writes, "in order to attend to the existence of something else, a natural object, a person in need." Here is a passage that nicely spells out Murdoch's perspective:

> I am looking out of my window in an anxious and resentful state of mind, oblivious of my surroundings, brooding perhaps on some damage done to my prestige. Then suddenly I observe a hovering kestrel. In a moment everything is altered. The brooding self with its hurt vanity has disappeared. There is nothing now but kestrel. And when I return to thinking of the other matter it seems less important. (p. 82)

The *world* has returned, and it has done so at precisely the same moment that the autobiographical self and its narrative have "disappeared."

In a related vein, Ciaran Benson, in his book, *The Absorbed Self* (1993), speaks of "centredness" in this context, "a type of experience in which selves are described as merging, fusing, uniting with, or simply becoming other than themselves" (p. 2). Unselfconscious absorption of the sort my mother would experience thus involves the "non-deployment of I" (p. 83), such that my "'location' is centred in and about the object rather than on my own moods and emotions" (p. 97). This "non-deployment," however, isn't complete—not, at least, when there is the kind of ecstatic absorption being considered. According to Benson, "While I am absorbed 'in the object,' there continues to be ... a 'residual awareness' of myself as spectator, listener or reader, an awareness which is a central logical requirement for its being aesthetic" (p. 97). I'm not sure that such putative self-awareness is the best way of describing what's going on in instances like these. Indeed, returning to the idea of "location," it may seem that "I" have become part of "the cloud I am gazing at, or the blackbird I am listening to" (p. 99). In this respect, I "disappear." Paraphrasing Murdoch, there is nothing but cloud, nothing but blackbird.

My own way of framing these issues is to invoke in yet another way "the priority of the Other," seeing in mysticism, especially, a profound and important challenge to the legacy of the self (Freeman, 2004, 2014a). Murdoch's preferred vehicle of unselfing is great art, which:

> teaches us how real things can be looked at and loved without being seized and used, without being appropriated into the greedy organism of the self. This exercise of *detachment* is difficult and valuable whether the thing contemplated is a human being or the root of a tree or the vibration of a colour or a sound. (1970, p. 64)

Why is it so difficult? The reason is all too clear: "We are anxiety-ridden animals. Our minds are continually active, fabricating an anxious, usually self-preoccupied ... *veil* which partially conceals the world" (p. 82).

We are also *narrating* animals, and following Sartwell (2000), this is part of the problem too. Narrative anxiety "infects every aspect of life," and it is imperative, he insists, that we devise ways of halting the infection. Not unlike Murdoch, Sartwell seeks to remind us that,

> The deepest human needs and their satisfactions ... take the form precisely of a letting-go, or a languorous lapse into silence. We take pleasure in eating a good meal, but not because it leads us toward salvation, or even because it leads us toward happiness considered as a property of a whole life, but because it calls us into a present enjoyment wherein the imaginative reconstruction of the temporal flow is suspended. (p. 67)

Letting go, in short, brings one beyond narrative, or least that dimension of it that is tied to the autobiographical self. As I acknowledged in the previous chapter, my mother was unable to do this through my imploring her to do so. Indeed, insofar as letting go implies something that one does intentionally, purposefully, I don't know that she could ever do this. Instead, she had to be *let* go, we might say, unselfed by precisely those objects and experiences that called her out of herself.

***

It is possible that the task of achieving the state Murdoch and Sartwell are considering is made easier in dementia. With the removal, or at least the diminution, of the "self-preoccupied veil" that conceals the world, perhaps the world can more readily be *un*concealed (see Heidegger, 1971). It is even possible that the ontological/spiritual identity I mentioned earlier is further realized in this condition; perhaps there is some sort of opening into the "beyond"—the world beyond narrative and verbal articulation more generally—that can allow this to occur. Murdoch speaks in this context of the "spiritual role" of music, for instance, and how art, more generally, "pierces the veil and gives sense to the notion of a reality which lies beyond appearance" (p. 86). She also speaks of the connection between such experience and mysticism, which, on her account, is nothing more and nothing less than "a non-dogmatic essentially unformulated faith in the reality of the Good, occasionally connected with experience" (p. 72).

I need to be clear about this. I certainly do not wish to equate the kind of experience that can emerge in the context of dementia with mystical experience. This would be to romanticize dementia and to pathologize mysticism. Nevertheless, it may be that each, in their unique ways of moving beyond narrative, offers a kind of deliverance, a reprieve from the anxiety and pressure of the autobiographical self. Whether this process of autobiographical unselfing has the redemptive outcome we had been hoping for, only time would tell. For the time being, we would have to work together to find resources, internal as well as external, to help my mother through some difficult days. This meant finding "objects" that could foster the process of unselfing, and thereby allow her some measure of felt connection to the world. We had already caught glimpses of such experiences—music and children, good meals and glasses of wine—but these were somewhat fleeting. Eventually, there would be others, more sustained and more intense, owing, no doubt, to the progression of the disease.

One in particular stands out. It was one of those fall days in New England that demanded your attention. Mom and I decided to take a drive up a country road, toward Mt. Wachusett, which offers vistas of the lush valley below, the mountains of New Hampshire to the north, and on a crystal-clear day like that one, the Boston skyline. I tuned the car stereo to a local classical station. Up we went, climbing the road to the mountain, music playing, the sky blue, the leaves beginning to turn, shaking loose, skittering across the road. She was transfixed.

"Beautiful."

"It must be peak now."

"Such a pretty road."

"Beautiful, beautiful day."

"What a day."

"Spectacular day for a ride like this."

"What a spectacular, beautiful day."

It wasn't actually peak yet, but no matter. For her, it was close enough.

It's not easy to make sense of these kinds of utterances. There were times when words would simply spill out, appropriately; even later, after the disease had intensified, she often knew what to say—that is, what's generally said—in a given context. "Reading, picking up," the sort of answers I mentioned earlier. She was a good talker. I don't mean to suggest that she was lying at these times. Indeed, she could no doubt comfort herself with the fact that, in her mind, she had indeed been reading and picking up. But it was sometimes difficult to know what her words actually meant. This was true of our ride together that beautiful fall day. At times, it was like playing a record that keeps on skipping.

But there were other times too, when the kaleidoscope of colors before her, suffused, no doubt, with her own distant, New England memories, washed upon her in ecstatic waves, giving her a measure of reprieve from the onslaught of days following one another in their sameness. Her repetition in these moments followed the movement of these waves, and each statement she made, even if exactly the same as the one uttered the minute before, was brand new. For a moment or two—and I assure you, only for a moment or two—I envied her. That day, I really couldn't *be* there, with the world, like she was. I kept moving in and out, between the welter of colors and this or that issue that had to be thought about, between the incredible vistas and my mother's fate. That day, for a few hours, she was … happy. Or something like it. I can't pretend to know exactly where she was, but wherever it was, it did seem to bring her a kind of oneness, a full immersion in the world, untouched by all the chattering stuff inside our heads that keep us from being present to things.

Here was a classic example of what I had come to refer to as "dementia's tragic promise" (Freeman, 2008a). What would the future bring? Would there be more of the same? Whatever might happen going forward, I was glad, privileged even, to share these moments with her, tragic though they ultimately were. There could still be joy then, rapture, of a sort I had never really seen in her before, measured as she was before dementia hit. But what she was able to experience at these times wasn't just a function of "disinhibition," operative though it probably was. It was a function of truly undivided attention of a sort that most of us only seldom, if ever, experience.

***

Simone Weil (1952/1997) has expressed what would seem to be an impossible wish. "May I disappear in order that those things that I see become perfect in their beauty from the very fact that they are no longer things I see." As she goes on to clarify, "I do not in the least wish that this created world should fade from my view, but that it should no longer be to me personally that it shows itself." Weil knew that, strictly speaking, this cannot happen: "When I am in any place, I disturb the silence of heaven and earth by my breathing and the beating of my heart." The aim nevertheless remains: "To see a landscape as it is when I am not there" (p. 37)—in short, to "unself" oneself, as Murdoch (1970) had put it, to the greatest possible extent in order to engage, and be engaged by, reality.

Through no effort of her own, my mother was able to do something very much like what Weil had wished for. In keeping with what was said earlier, she was still "there" to some degree; if she wasn't, there wouldn't, and couldn't, be the rapture. But it's as if she were brought to a kind of limit point, to a state of being that had been radically emptied of self but still able to see, hear, feel what was there in the world. Simone Weil might have envied her too.

Whether wittingly or not, my mother had given herself over to the world at these moments, such that it could appear, and reappear, in all of its bounty and freshness and goodness. She was truly awestruck, and rather than taking pause and reflecting on the spectacle before her, she became awestruck once more, taken aback by what the world could be, by what the world *is,* if we could attend enough to truly encounter it.

It could be that I'm romanticizing or overvaluing the events of that day and other days when similar experiences arose. I actually referred to her in a piece I wrote at the time as "the Buddha," living in the moment, utterly attentive to what is, immensely grateful for being there, in the world's presence. This is a stretch, I know; she had hardly cultivated this way of being in the world, and the nature of her ecstatic response was undoubtedly of a substantially different kind than what we would find among virtuosos like the Buddha himself. And yet, I don't want to discount this connection, for there were moments during this strange, occasionally wondrous phase, when my mother, largely shorn of ego and desire, became transfixed enough by the spectacle before her as to call out in prayerful joy the great good fortune of being there to witness it and to let it fill her as it could. She realized something in these moments, and although she couldn't possibly have articulated what it was, there is every reason, I believe, to trust her "judgments" at the time.

Beautiful.

Say it again: *beautiful.*

And again: *beautiful.*

Always there. Always renewed. She clearly felt that.

Some of the repetition I witnessed that day was merely a function of the fact that she couldn't remember what she had said moments before. But it wasn't only that; there was a kind of redoubling at work too, an intensification, an underscoring of what she was seeking and feeling and being. This suggests that things can be revealed, even in the dreaded and dreadful depths of dementia, that are vitally significant and supremely real. What a gift it was to be with her in moments like these. Unprecedented, and unparalleled. How strange, and tragic, and beautiful.

***

Even now, I don't know how to make sense of all this. But I seem to need to, somehow; I guess that's the psychologist in me. Earlier, I broached the idea of an ontological or spiritual identity that may continue to exist even after autobiographical identity has been left behind. In discussing this distinction with a colleague, I was introduced to a similar distinction made by Antonio Damasio in *The Feeling of What Happens* (1999). During the course of development, Damasio suggests, there is a movement from a "core self" to an "autobiographical self." In regard to the former, he writes:

> You know that you are conscious, you feel that you are in the act of knowing, because the subtle imaged account that is now flowing in the stream of your organism's thoughts exhibits the knowledge that your proto-self has been changed by an object that has just become salient in the mind. You know you exist because the narrative exhibits you as a protagonist in the act of knowing. You rise above the sea level of knowing, transiently but incessantly, as a *felt* core self, renewed again and again, thanks to anything that comes from outside the brain into its sensory machinery or anything that comes from the brain's memory stores toward sensory, motor, or autonomic recall. You know it is *you*

seeing because the story depicts a character—you—doing the seeing. (pp. 171–172)

Damasio refers in this context to T. S. Eliot's *Four Quartets*, which spoke of a music "heard so deeply that it is not heard at all," and which states that "you are the music while the music lasts." Eliot, Damasio surmises, was apparently thinking of "the fleeting moment in which a deep knowledge can emerge—a union, or incarnation, as he called it" (p. 172). Damasio's core self thus bears within it a spiritual possibility, connected with the very ineffable nature of "being the music"—or the great-grandchild or glass of good wine—"anything that comes from outside the brain into its sensory machinery."

It should be noted that, for Damasio, the core self is itself bound up with narrative, albeit of a wordless sort:

Knowing springs to life in the story, it inheres in the newly constructed neural pattern that constitutes the nonverbal account. You hardly notice the storytelling because the images that dominate the mental display are those of the things of which you are now conscious—the objects you see or hear—rather than those that swiftly constitute the feeling of you in the act of knowing. (p. 172)

It is difficult to know what to make of this conceptualization. While narrative, or "narrativity," may well be a precondition of sorts for achieving the kind of "union" about which Damasio speaks, it is not entirely clear that "storytelling" is involved. Be that as it may, this notion of a core self, of a self that is "renewed again and again" through its encounter with the *Other-than-self*, remains an important one.

In the healthy mind, Damasio continues, something does in fact last after the (proverbial) music is gone:

In complex organisms such as ours, equipped with vast memory capacities, the fleeting moments of knowledge in which we discover our existence are facts that can be committed to memory, be properly categorized, and be related to other memories that pertain both to the past and to the anticipated future. The consequence of that complex learning operation is the development of autobiographical memory, an aggregate of dispositional records of who we have been physically and of who we have usually been behaviorally, along with records of who we plan to be in the future. We can enlarge this aggregate memory and refashion it as we go through a lifetime. When certain personal records are made explicit in reconstructed images, as needed, in smaller or greater quantities, they become the *autobiographical self.* (pp. 172–173)

Whether Damasio is right to speak of aggregates and records is open to question; his terminology bespeaks a kind of substantialism that runs counter to much current thinking about autobiographical memory and the autobiographical self. Nevertheless, the distinction at hand between the core self and the autobiographical self is a useful one, in regard to both development and the process of decline as it is observed in dementia and related maladies. In the early stages of development, Damasio suggests, there may be "little more than reiterated states of core self." With continued experience, however, "autobiographical memory grows and the autobiographical self can be deployed" (p. 175). The process of decline, in turn, moves in the reverse direction: "When the loss of memory for past events is marked enough to compromise autobiographical records, the autobiographical self is gradually extinguished and extended consciousness collapses. This happens in advance of the subsequent collapse of core consciousness" (p. 209). If Damasio is right, therefore, the core self remains—for a time—after the demise of the autobiographical self.

I am still not sure how well this set of ideas applies to my mother's situation. What I can say is that this phase of my mother's life, permeated though it was by loss, also opened up new possibilities of experience for her. Whether this represents "gain" is open to question. There is no question, though, that her very decline, vis-à-vis the autobiographical self, brought with it unprecedented moments of grace and respite, moments in which she was carefree, present to the world, able to feel its bounty and be nourished by it. On a given day, this could happen again and again and again, the erasure of the moment recently passed opening the way to a brand new one, a never-before one, bursting forth with the force of a revelation.

Was she "lucky" to have had these moments come her way, unsought and unbidden? Seen from the standpoint of a normally functioning, dementia-free person, no; her ecstasies were largely the consequence of a diseased brain. At the same time, I wouldn't want to underplay the depth of her feeling and the *reality* that made it possible. Fleeting though these experiences were, they yielded something not unlike what Simone Weil had wished for and not unlike what many of us seek, in one way or another, when, burdened by our lives, we try to divest ourselves of all that holds us back from unadulterated presence. In the end, I don't think this is cause for envy. But it is cause for a kind of quiet celebration, of what life can bring, what life can *be*, even amidst devastation and decline.

It is also cause for a more capacious view of Alzheimer's. "Alzheimer's disease," Cohen and Eisdorfer (2001) write, "is a cruel disorder. However, no matter how devastating it is, the essential humanity of the 'person-turned-patient' remains …. As the disease progresses," they continue, "there is little or no hope of recovery of memory. But people do not consist of memory alone. People have needs as well as feelings, imagination, desires, drives, will, and moral being" (p. 22). Well said.

I want to take this basic line of thinking one step further. As my mother's situation during this phase suggests, it's not just a matter of what "remains" amidst the devastation and loss—important though that is to recognize—but also of what may be *revealed*, about both self and world. Again, I don't think she herself could have articulated the nature of such revelation. For one, that would have required a level of reflective consciousness that was likely beyond her. For another, these experiences vanished as quickly as they arrived. There would be no preserving them, no "catching" them, and consequently, there would be no way of extracting the substance of what they may have revealed. Nevertheless, I think it's fair to say that the very extremity of my mother's condition had ushered in something new, something that not only testifies to what remains but also what grows, bursts forth, in ways that surpass some of the limits of ordinary life. There is real promise in such experience, tragic though it is, and it's important that it be recognized, and painful though it may be, welcomed.

CHAPTER 4

DISLOCATION

I still believe what I said at the end of the previous chapter. What I had earlier termed "dementia's tragic promise" had in fact been realized on some level, and I believe that, at its apex, like that trek up the mountain in the fall, aspects of being in the world were revealed that were, that *are*, eminently real.

But the promise, like the leaves, would begin to fade. Later that fall, my mother was often agitated, and even went on several "rampages" (as they were described by staff at Tatnuck Park). The food was awful, and she let everyone around her in the dining room know it. She yelled at people, for who knows what infraction, loudly and venomously enough that one of her very few friends, an older Jewish man whose wife was dying and who would "kibitz" with her in language colorfully sprinkled with the Yiddish they both knew and loved, had scolded her for her rudeness and told her to "act like a lady." And then, yet again (and again), there were the "thefts": her bangle, her wallet, her keys, her glasses, her ring, her watch.

"They were right on my dresser! *Mark*, I put them in the same place every night!"

When I would find them tucked in a drawer in the folds of a sweater or underneath a tangle of socks and stockings, she was utterly mystified. *How did they get there?* Not for a split second did the idea cross her mind that she could have done it; it was literally inconceivable. As for why the ever-present "they" would take her beaten, old watch but leave a new piece of jewelry behind, the reason was simple enough: They didn't have a blessed clue about what was of value and what was not. "Those people, what do they know?" Everything had an explanation, and the explanation inevitably had to do with what had been taken from her. She was right about this, of course: So much in her life, once full and present, had gone missing.

One time, I got a call at work and was told that I had two choices: either come and get Mom for the weekend or she would be sent to the local psychiatric hospital, probably for three weeks or so, where, if all went well, they would concoct a pharmacological cocktail that would take enough wind out of her paranoid, rageful sails that she could return "home." We took her for the weekend, and she was basically fine. She did ask, "Whose house is this?" at one point, probably because she was sitting in a room where she rarely sits. So we took a little walk through the kitchen and into the dining room, where many a meal had taken place and many bottles of wine consumed.

Oh, yes. *Here*.

"Geez, ma," I said. "You had me worried there for a minute."

Things stayed fairly calm for a while, but then the theft fantasies reemerged, and the yelling and rage. A new medicine would take the edge off things, but it would also leave her more at sea. It was difficult to know what she did all day. She could still do some reading, but judging by the stack of books in her apartment, she didn't do much. So the pile grew. She did straighten up her apartment occasionally, but not often. And there were the sporadic crossword puzzles, partially finished, a group activity now and then, and when the spirit struck her, some small talk with her fellow residents. But there were also long spells of nothingness, times when she would sit in a chair or lie in bed, and just … be. She began to wear the same clothes, day in and day out. Her hair was often unkempt, scraggly. She started to shuffle when she walked. Dosage would have to be recalibrated; we worked to find some middle ground between her paranoid rage and this dreadful void. But this was also a new phase.

Even after Mom was taken off the medication that was sapping her spirit, she frequently remained dulled and lost. I mean this quite literally. One day, when I stopped by her apartment, the telephone directory was open to the page that included her name and number. At the top of the page, she had scrawled her name. The ink was heavy and dark, the "F" circled, and in the column of names, hers was underlined, roughly and repeatedly. I will not pretend to know exactly what was going through her mind at the time, but there can be little doubt that she was trying to find what seemed to be irretrievably lost. She was just "foggy" much of the time.

"I don't know what I *did* all day," she would say. "Got to get my head on straight. I have to get started, get my head on straight, start getting into a program of some sort."

She had a lingering desire to *resume*, to return, somehow, to her old self and her old life, the one that had included schedules and routines, "taking care of things." My mother seemed to have a memory of having *had* a narrative, of having lived the sort of life that would include schedules and routines, but the narrative itself was distant, a sort of vaporous image that would occasionally waft into view, only to be abandoned in a matter of moments when she would return to simply sitting and being, staring off into space. Vacant.

There was something of a silver lining, even amidst this deepening emptiness. It was icy cold in New England at the time. For years, wintry weather like this would bring out my mother's anger and resentment over the fact that she was up in the frigid north rather than down in Florida, where she had been "just fine" until we stuck our noses into things and insisted that she move. "Sorry, Ma, we really wanted you near us." If we were lucky, her rage would dissipate. But things had become very different. The "good" news was that, even though she still couldn't stand the cold, not once did she mention going to Florida. The not-so-good news, of course, was bound up with this same fact. The resentment was largely gone, the insult, the felt impotence. I can't say that we missed her seasonal tirades; those could be rough. But we were beginning to miss *her*, or at least that version of her that had so long been with us.

***

I still wondered what my mother did all day. I know that she had started to sleep more. For a while, she was also eating more, lots more, as the 30 or so pounds she'd put on testified. She would eat whatever was put in front of her, forkful after forkful, in a steady, droning rhythm until it was gone. Buffets were particularly dangerous; she had no sense of how much she had consumed, and was ever ready to "try that other dish," even if she'd already tried it. Eventually, though, she would reject much of the food offered to her; it was too sweet, too salty, whatever. During one dinner, she complained endlessly about how tough the chicken was, how you could barely cut it. Little surprise: She was trying to cut through bone with her knife turned upside down. Funny. (Sort of.) Even upon making some headway with the chicken, she complained that it was dry and overcooked, despite the fact that it was actually quite juicy.

I once heard a joke about a group of older women sitting at a dining room table, much like the one where Mom and others took their meals. Midway through the meal, the maître d (or its assisted living equivalent) came by the table and sweetly asked, "Is anything OK?" Not far from the way it was.

Complaining about the food became something of a pastime. This was, in part, a function of her self-styled image of being something of a connoisseur, a maven, and in part a function of her negativity, her newfound inclination to find fault whenever and wherever she could. One story really stands out. Our daughter Justine worked at Tatnuck Park for a while as a member of the waitstaff, and on the day in question, rhubarb pie was on the menu for dessert. Knowing that Grandma would almost certainly start bitching about the pie, Justine, whose incredible posture Mom took special pride in, decided to perform a little experiment.

"*I* baked it, Grandma," she said. "What do you think?"

My mother didn't say a word. And then, as Justine walked away, she muttered, "She can't bake, but she's got a hell of a posture!"

Fortunately, the sorrow and the rage could be interrupted every now and then. Lord knows we needed it.

***

Things had begun darkening for my mother; there was very little at this point that was "right" or "good." Rhubarb pie aside, the only thing that came close food-wise were desserts. The result was that she had taken to asking for multiples—some pie, then maybe some ice cream, perhaps even something else after that. So she continued to get larger and larger. Occasionally, she could see what was happening and bemoaned it; hardly any of her clothes fit her, she was having more difficulty breathing, and she'd been getting backaches from carrying such a big load. But when the waitstaff tried to dissuade her from eating that second or third dessert, she would become enraged and insist that she be served. I sat down with her once and we drew up a contract of sorts, that both she and I would sign, mainly geared toward lessening her dessert intake. It went fine; we signed and that was that. The contract was to be kept right at her place at the dinner table to remind her of our agreement. But she balked at even this, despite the fact that her signature was right there before her. Her response was telling, indeed: The signature was forged. Phenomenologically speaking, she was speaking the truth. The person she was, then and there, didn't sign that paper; someone else did.

There were still some lighthearted moments. Shortly after signing that dessert contract, I asked her if she remembered what the contract was about.

"Yeah," she said, "it's to say I won't be a pig!"

When I asked her whether she knew how old she was, she admitted that she didn't know. "We could do what you do with trees!" I offered.

Her rejoinder was swift: "Count my wrinkles?!"

And when we talked for the umpteenth time about our Thanksgiving plans and she lamented the fact that she couldn't seem to hold on to anything ("What a head," she said), I told her it was OK. "You've got a memory problem, Ma. You're still capable of enjoyment, you just can't remember some of it."

"Can't enjoy it twice," she replied.

For a brief moment, the old, familiar "she" was back: a self, a narrative self, with some awareness of the world she has come to inhabit.

There also remained some moments when my mother was able to lose herself in such a way as to yield some pleasure. I took her to a couple of concerts that she really seemed to enjoy. Around the same time, she told me about how she had stood at her living room window and watched a couple of squirrels running and chasing each other through the trees. She was still transfixed by beautiful days too, but she had grown less capable of feeling the kind of oneness that she had felt before. Such oneness, we noted, still requires a self, in enough contact with the world as to be able to draw nourishment from it. Murdoch's "unselfing," therefore, is only partial; to be fully present to the world, there needs to be someone there to witness and savor it, an *I* who sees and feels. It's a matter of relation. As this I begins to lose its foothold in reality, there comes to be less world to witness, and less nourishment, less sustenance. Is that why Mom had put on so much weight? Maybe she was taking in what pleasure she could. I don't know. What I do know is that her ecstatic moments were growing fewer and farther between. We knew we would need to work hard to find things that could reach her.

***

Beyond some extra sleeping and eating, it remained hard to know what Mom did all day.

"Are you bored?" I asked once.

"No, not really."

"Are there things you'd like to be doing?"

"No, I can't really think of anything."

That really says it all.

***

It is commonly understood that personal identity is, in significant part, a function of memory. The view long shared by philosophers, psychologists, and others is that the very idea of identity—which, in broad terms, can be understood as the experience of one's continuity in time, even amidst all the changes one undergoes—relies upon the "preservation" of the past in and through memory and the persistence of this past into the present. More recently, as was suggested earlier, it has come to be understood by some that personal identity is a function not just of memory but also of narrative, the very sense of our own singularity and particularity emerging through story, both lived and told (e.g., Freeman, 1993; McAdams, 1997; McAdams, Josselson, & Lieblich, 2006).

Along these lines, philosopher Paul Ricoeur (1991a) writes, "my life" may be understood "as a story in its nascent state ... an *activity and a passion in search of a narrative.*" It is for this reason that he wishes "to grant to experience as such a virtual narrativity which stems, not from the projection of literature onto life, but which constitutes a genuine demand for narrative" (p. 29). We are "entangled" in stories, Ricoeur insists; narrating, of the sort we do when we pause to tell those larger stories that comprise our lives, is a "secondary process" that is "grafted" onto this entanglement. In this sense, the actual stories we tell about ourselves are seen as a continuation and extension of those "unspoken stories" we routinely live. "Our life, when then embraced in a single glance, appears to us as the field of a constructive activity, borrowed from narrative understanding, by which we attempt to discover and not simply to impose from outside the *narrative identity which constitutes us*" (p. 32; see also Ricoeur, 1992; Freeman, 2013; McAdams & McLean, 2013). Ricoeur has done well to articulate the interrelationship between the "narrativity" that is part and parcel of life itself, the actual narratives we tell about our lives, and the narrative identity that grows out of the two.

In my mother's case, this interrelationship had become severely compromised. "Our life" was no longer *her* life, and the "attempt to discover ... the narrative identity which constitutes us" was only minimally operative at this stage. Indeed, her life, to the extent that it could be "embraced in a single glance," yielded something quite different than the panoramic landscape of the past we might ordinarily see. By all indications, it yielded a kind of desolate tundra, a vast expanse of nothingness.

At these times, Mom would have no idea whatsoever where she was or who she was. For a while, this would sometimes happen upon her waking from a nap and finding everything around her unfamiliar and strange. It's hard to imagine what her world must have been like. Occasionally, I wake up in the middle of the night, in a hotel room, for instance, and have no idea where I am or how I got there. After a few weird moments, I remember and go back to sleep. But this is exactly what my mother couldn't do. It wasn't like being in a new place—that can be interesting and exciting. Instead, she said, it was like being in "another world."

This began to happen more regularly, and not just from post-nap confusion. In a distinct sense, "Where *am* I?" would become fused with "Where am *I*?" The result could be sheer panic. There was another result too. Mom needed to find me immediately, and she sometimes called, frantically trying to reach me. One night, with the help of one of the aides, she called in a panic and told me in a shaky voice that she was at Holy Cross (where I work).

"I doubt that, Ma," I said. "You're at home, at Tatnuck Park."

She then asked the aide where she was.

"You're in your own apartment, where you've been living," the aide assured her.

"Well, that's news to me."

My voice calmed her down. "You'll be OK, Ma. This happens once in a while, but eventually, things start to look familiar again. So just take it easy. I'll be over in a little while."

These rescue efforts became quite a heavy responsibility. Not only did my family and I live close by and need to be "on call," but my mother's very sense of location, in a recognizable world, had come to depend in part on me. I could help return her to the world and to herself, such as it was, at least for a while.

One day, I stopped by her apartment to say hello. Mom was sitting on a comfortable sofa by the fireplace. As I walked toward her, I could see that she was anxious and uncomfortable.

"It's a good thing you showed up when you did," she said.

"Why?" I asked.

She had absolutely no idea what she was doing there. "Do I stay here?" she asked.

"Yes, you live here; you have for a couple of years."

None of it was familiar. "I don't know where I am. I don't know who I am." This was a remarkable insight. For a brief moment, she is still able to reflect, to take her own confused experience as an object of thought. But there is no connectedness, no narrative through-line. She was truly "in the moment." But without some semblance of a narrative self to condition and guide the moment, there can only be a kind of perpetual onslaught of presents, devoid of pastness and futurity alike and thereby essentially deprived of meaning, deprived of reality. She seemed to know this. Had I not arrived when I did, she went on to say, she might have screamed.

CHAPTER 4

Through it all, "she"—whatever remained of her identity—could sense that something was radically amiss, that there was something missing, that something that was once there no longer was.

***

In episodes like the ones I have been recounting, there would seem to be little in the way of autobiographical memory or narrative. Nothing was recognizable, including herself. She was inhabiting a world without a discernible history, without traces of a knowable past. It is against the backdrop of this situation that I referred to "life without narrative" (2008b) in a piece I wrote at the time. Against those who argue that we don't really live narratives, but simply impose them after the fact onto the past—the supposition therefore being that "real life" is narrative-free—I argued that a narrative-free life, far from necessarily leading in the direction of the real, could lead instead to the void. My mother's life showed this with painful clarity. As for why she had moved from the ecstatic, quasi-mystical form of being divested of narrative we encountered earlier to this more chaotic, disturbing form, it seemed to have something to do with her increasingly tenuous connection to reality itself. Alongside dislocation was derealization, and in place of the rapture of belonging in and to the world, there was a profound sense of having been exiled from it.

I did go on to offer a qualification to this notion of life without narrative. Even though much of my mother's memory had been erased, there still remained some sense of identity. This is why, even after a panic-stricken and terrifying episode of dislocation, she could step back from this very dislocatedness and say something about it. "Oh my god," she would say. "Oh my god." "Oh my god." Then, there might be an additional lament, in the form of a Yiddish phrase her mother would sometimes utter: "Oh, what becomes of a person."

But who, I had asked, was this "she" who had been stunned into disbelief? What was it that led her to retain this vestigial sense, albeit damaged, of identity? And where does this "myth," as I called it (Freeman, 2009), come from? There is a puzzle here. Even in the face of the demise of memory and narrative, residing in a world in which everything could appear alien and unfamiliar, there was an acknowledgment of this very alienness and unfamiliarity as well as the recognition that she herself was to "blame." That's not all; there also remained a fairly strong wall of defenses. When I told her that her lapses had occurred before, she was either completely mystified, finding it inconceivable, or positively annoyed, as in, "I think I would *know* if this happened before." This bespeaks not only a vestigial sense of identity, but a relatively strong one at that. Sometimes she appeared to herself to be "dumb," "mindless." (Those are her words, not mine.) But there were other times when she was ready to blast us for even *thinking* that she could forget these harsh episodes. In her case, at least, the myth of identity was stubborn indeed. Again, why?

***

William James, in *The Principles of Psychology* (1890/1950), suggested that personal identity has something to do with the capacity to identify the different "objects" one encounters, including one's previous states of consciousness, as "one's own." His conception of identity thus relies on memory, on the *presence* of memories, of past selves, continuous with the present self and thus able to be identified as "mine." James speaks of a "warmth" and "intimacy" in this context, even an "aroma" and an "echo."

> And by a natural consequence, we shall assimilate them to each other and to the warm and intimate self we now feel within us as we think, and separate them as a collection from whatever selves have not this mark, much as out of a herd of cattle let loose for the winter on some wide western prairie the owner picks out and sorts together when the time for the round-up comes in the spring, all the beasts on which he finds his own particular brand.

> The various members of the collection thus set apart are felt to belong with each other whenever they are thought at all. The animal warmth, etc., is their herd-mark, the brand from which they can never more escape. (pp. 333–334)

A classic statement of identity, and on some level, a compelling one. "And thus it is," James continues,

> that Peter, awakening in the same bed with Paul, and recalling what both had in mind before they went to sleep, reidentifies and appropriates the "warm" ideas as his, and is never tempted to confuse them with those cold and pale-appearing ones which he ascribes to Paul. As well might he confound Paul's body, which he only sees, with his own body, which he sees but also feels. Each of us when he awakens says, Here's the

same old self again, just as he says, Here's the same old bed, the same old room, the same old world. (p. 334)

But there is a curious fact that emerges in cases like my mother's—namely, that when *she* awakened, she couldn't say, "Here's the same old bed, the same old room, the same old world." She did tend to remember the things that were in her apartment, and she also remembered Debbie and me, but the apartment itself was completely unfamiliar. It's as if she were experiencing a kind of montage of the familiar and the unfamiliar, of things that had been an enduring enough part of her past to be retained and things that had no enduringness at all. I guess that's what she was too: a split identity-montage, comprising felt continuities and radical discontinuities, spheres of self-familiarity and spheres of self-alienation. It's like being in another world, she had said. She knew this and felt it and could speak about it. So even in the ostensible absence of memories, such that virtually nothing was familiar (except some of her old furniture and me and my immediate family), the sense of identity remained.

It's very curious. My presence at times like these was a mixed bag. On the one hand, I could calm her down, help her return to some semblance of reality. But at the very moment I did so, she could become acutely conscious of what had been lost. I suppose it was better than panic, and I suppose it was better than the utter void she sometimes fell into. But it was extremely disturbing in its own right, entailing a kind of existential liminality, a state of being in-between presence and absence—or put another way, a state of being wherein there is both the absence of presence, the absence of tangible memorial touchstones, and the presence of absence, the felt pressure and pain of there being something missing. Identity *in absentia*, as it were.

***

In the aforementioned piece, "Life Without Narrative" (2008b), I constructed a corrective to my earlier thoughts regarding dementia's tragic promise. In that context, I held out the somewhat perverse hope that as the disease progressed, there would be less memory and less self, and consequently, a state of selfless oneness. That promise proved to be short-lived. Oneness would be replaced by nothingness, tragic promise by tragic demise.

But this story needs some correction too. Although I did offer a qualification to the notion of life without narrative by virtue of the fact that my mother could sometimes become aware of her situation, conscious of its very nothingness, this consciousness seemed to be a kind of weak layover that would fade away in due time, like an ember that would suddenly flare up and then die down again, eventually to be extinguished. But it didn't happen this way. Even amidst the further deterioration of my mother's memory, short-term and long-term alike, significant elements of identity remained. These were most visibly manifested in her lamentations regarding her sorry state, the "Oh my gods" that would pour forth when she struggled, whether over walking or thinking. So I ask again: Who exactly was it who felt this frustrated sense of loss, who had somehow retained a memory, however indistinct, of her own integral self? More to the point still: Given the ostensible absence of narrative, of a narrative view of her life, how might we account for this vestigial sense of identity, damaged though it had become?

Things were changing in ways that were often confusing. I wanted to try to better understand what was going on, so I started taking more notes, recording more of her words. At the time, I didn't know what I would do with them, but I knew I wanted to keep them, preserve them. Preserve her.

***

"It's not even a nightmare," my mother said of her life in early January 2008. "I don't know *what* it is." Later that same day, she asked, "Am I going to get up and get dressed and join the modern world, or am I going to turn around and go back to bed?"

The following week, we received a call from the nurse at Tatnuck Park. Mom was in the sunroom, where residents put together puzzles and the like, and had apparently taken off all her clothes. Time for bed. Someone was able to put a sweater on her, and at least she had her panties back on. Then, after rerobing, she went to dinner, as usual.

***

"I'll probably see you tomorrow, Ma," I said one time upon leaving.
"Oh?" she said. "That would be great."
"We're neighbors," I explained.
"Neighbors?"
"Well, we live pretty close to you."
"But I wasn't sure *how* close."
"I'm in Worcester. You're in Worcester."
Around this time, questions began to abound.
"What town is this?"

"How long have I lived here?"

"How far away do you live?"

"Have I ever been here before?"

After a tour around Worcester a few months later to see her old apartments (she had two), she was taken aback by how unfamiliar everything was.

"Yeah, there are a lot of things that you're forgetting these days," I said (unnecessarily). "But you know, you're lucky, Ma. Some people forget people too."

"If I didn't remember you," she said, "I'd really be ready for the gas pipe."

"Well, not really," I responded (*extra* unnecessarily), "because you wouldn't know it." Ugh. Why did I need to say that?

***

We decided to go to her favorite Chinese restaurant one day. *That's bound to be familiar*, I thought. We could get her favorite dishes too.

"Is this Chinese food?" she asked when she began eating.

(Yes.)

"It doesn't *taste* like Chinese food!"

"I don't know what to tell you, Ma. It's Chinese food." What about the restaurant? Maybe she would recognize that. "Does this place look familiar to you?" I asked.

"Not really."

Trivial though this little episode may appear, it was scary. It was strange that Mom's memory of Chinese food—her beloved eggplant with garlic sauce—would last longer than her memory of important people in her life. But that's how it was. Was this a momentary lapse? Or did it augur something more permanent?

***

This is another feature of dementia—or at least Mom's version of it—that's worth noting. Memories would come and go. We could sometimes feel that she had taken a precipitous and ostensibly permanent fall downhill, only to find her "better" the next day or week. Likewise, we could sometimes gather a shred of hope when she did something that seemed to indicate improvement of some sort, even while knowing that it was probably illusory. Reviewing my notes therefore took me by surprise sometimes. How could she have said that then? Hadn't she already moved beyond that phase?

I have tried to tell a *story* in this book, one with a discernible trajectory, discrete chapters, laid out in roughly chronological order. In doing so, I have told the truth as best I could. The reality of my mother's situation, however, was frequently quite messy—messier, at times, than this story might suggest. There *was* a trajectory. There *were* chapters, of a sort. But the trajectory wasn't smooth or seamless, and the chapters, while differentiable, sometimes bled into one another in unanticipated ways. As always, there are other ways I could have told this story. In addition, there are other ways of depicting what went on than in fluid, coherent, "big story" (Freeman, 2006) form. Following the efforts of Michael Bamberg and Alexandra Georgakopolou (Bamberg, 2006; Bamberg & Georgakopolou, 2008; Georgakopolou, 2007), among others, it was important to tell "small stories" alongside the larger one, stories happening in the context of real dialogue, in real time. This is one reason I have adopted the format I have, the breaks between sections serving to capture some of the brokenness and *in*coherence of what went on.

***

Mom and I went on to talk about family. "Do I have another son in Worcester?" she asked.

(No.)

"Where do my other sons live?"

"You have one in New Jersey."

"Ken," she said.

"And one in Albany."

"What's his name?"

"Bobby."

(Apologies, Bob; if it's any comfort, she would eventually forget all of our names.)

***

Another day, I got a phone call from the main desk: Mom was very confused, and wanted to speak to someone who knew her.

I called her and asked if she'd like me to come over, which she did.

(Yes.)

"I woke up from a nap, and my mind just went blank. It's never happened before."

"Well, Ma, actually it has, but you don't remember that it happened so it feels new to you."

I went over. When I arrived, I heard the story again.

"I woke up, and my mind was blank. It's never happened before."

"Well, it has happened before, Ma, but you have some memory problems so you don't remember having been there."

"I would remember if this had happened before!"

"Ma, all I can tell you is that it has, a number of times."

"This has happened before?"

"Yes, it has, but you don't remember it due to your memory."

"I have memory problems?"

"Yes, Ma; you have for quite a while, and you're taking some medicine for them—Namenda and Aricept."

"I didn't know what they were for."

"Well, actually you did, but you've forgotten; you've been on them for a couple of years now."

"So I have memory problems?"

"Yeah, Ma, you do."

"Oh, my god," she said. "God pity you." She called herself a "moron." And she apologized, again, and again.

***

My mother still knew, and loved, beautiful summer days.

"What a day," she said one day in July. "What a day." Again and again.

A better form of repetition! It had been a while since she had been in this more carefree and thankful mode.

"Thank you," she said, "for a beautiful day, for a beautiful ride, with beautiful people … whom I love very much, for picking me up and letting me interfere with your life."

Was this a joke? A little bout of passive aggressiveness? Whatever it was, it was a good day. We were thankful too.

But I was also "freaked," as I wrote in my notes at the time:

It's not all the stuff I have to do that gets to me; it's that there's absolutely nothing adequate that can be done. Every time I'm there, I stay for a while and then leave her in a pool of nothingness. And there's not a blessed thing to do about it …. Part of the problem is her very gratitude.

It's always a "treat" for me to be there. She comes up to me without saying a word and hugs me for dear life.

And when I ask her how she is, she frequently says, "Fine and dandy." That was Mom's mantra, at least when she felt things were going tolerably well. But there were reminders every day that it wasn't so. So the guilt and shame has absolutely nothing to do with her feeling abandoned or anything else; it had to do with the sheer, unending impotence I feel in the face of her situation.

***

Some moments of levity remained. I got a new pair of slick, waterproof shoes, and as the child I still was, I needed to show them off to Mom. "Check 'em out, Ma!"

"They do everything but scratch your back!" she said.

After some huffing and puffing during a leisurely walk with me, she cried out, "Gettin' to be an old bag!"

"You're not an old bag," I said. "You're an elderly woman."

"That's what an old bag is!"

There were also moments of insight. After one of her disoriented dislocations, when she had fretted about her brain, I asked whether I could get her a glass of wine. That sounded good to her, but then I became a bit hesitant.

"I don't know," I said. "You were complaining about your brain before."

"This way," she shot back, "I won't have the *sense* to complain!"

Yes, she sometimes seemed to know what was going on. Those brain problems were real, and they were clearly leading her down a troubled and troubling path.

"I don't have a brain," she said one day. She was exhausted too. "I don't feel like a hundred. I feel like a *thousand*." The obvious conclusion: "I'm going to need more than an apartment; I'm going to need assisted living."

Not a bad idea.

We didn't quite get senseless that day we shared some wine together. But it wasn't unusual for us to clink glasses, say "Cheers," and share a moment of quiet recognition of what had been going on. There was a kind of nostalgia in these moments, and it could dispel, even if temporarily, some of the feelings of loss that continued to come her way. And mine.

**

Some of the words I just shared date back to 2008. I wouldn't call that period a "hopeful" time. There had already been many disturbing moments, and in some vague, inarticulate way, my mother seemed to know that her situation was becoming more and more dire. Things would eventually intensify, though, and her sense of dislocation would no longer be limited to episodes but would instead come to permeate much of her life.

"Hi. Debbie? I'm at the apartment; and I'm trying to get hold of Mark … or you, to see about getting home. I came to get my hair done here, and I'm at my old apartment. I'm at the old apartment. Who lives here now? I don't know, but I'm … I'm right here in Worcester. And if you know the old apartment, you know where I am. OK? Thank you."

Following her call to Debbie was one to me.

"It's Mom. I'm at the old apartment here. I'm right here in Worcester, honey, but I don't know how to get in touch with you. I'm at my old apartment, so call me or come over. OK?"

And then another. "Debbie? I'm here at the … at the … near Mark's office here. I don't know where to get in touch with him or how to get in touch with you. Could one of you come over here and talk to me? I don't know if it's going to do any good."

Sometimes panic would reemerge; she would feel so untethered and lost that Debbie or I would have to race over to rescue her, like EMTs, help her relocate herself, bring her back to reality.

And so we did. We saw Mom often at this stage, but she didn't know it or feel it, and she would sometimes complain about being left alone.

"I see you multiple times a week, Ma."

"It's not enough."

She needed us more and more during this phase. She needed us there, with her. "I'm like a *child* now," she said. "I have to be put in a nursery with infants, to be watched."

"No, you're not; you're a full-grown adult."

"But mindless. Dumb." "Brainless," she said another time. "I don't have a brain anymore."

What a remarkable reversal. Early on, during the protest phase, she would scold me when she felt that I was treating her like a child. During this phase, she would tell me she is one. How things change.

***

New Year's Day 2009 seemed to mark a significant shift in Mom's way of being, though it's one that's difficult to specify with any precision. I called her late in the afternoon to see how she was feeling, and she immediately told a story about having woken up after five.

"I've lost big chunks of my memory," she said. "I've lost big chunks of my *life*."

"How long have I lived here?" she asked.

(I answer.)

"Three years?! Three years?! *Three years?!*"

(Yes.)

"Have you known that I was having some problems?"

(Yes.)

"My brain is mush." And you, my son, are here to witness it. "What you must feel like when you leave, to see your poor mother like this."

All of this was familiar on one level. Nearly every line she uttered had been uttered before. But there would eventually be a kind of "spaciousness" to her awareness, as Debbie put it at the time, one that suggested a new relationship to her situation. She was relatively devoid, it seemed, of deep feeling at this juncture. She didn't cry, which she sometimes did at times like this in the past; it was more cognitive. It also didn't seem particularly personal; it was more of a generic awareness of human loss, human demise, the fate of people.

She wondered, yet again, what was going on. She was perplexed, and badly needed an update.

"Well, Ma, there's really nothing new happening," I told her. "You've known about all this before."

"I've known about this?"

"Yes, we've spoken about it lots and lots of times."

"Oh my god. Oh my god." This time, the lament seemed different. It wasn't panicky, like it had been. It was almost as if there was a sense of resignation, in a "So, this is what it's come to" sort of way. There was also an element of mourning, though it wasn't quite clear of what.

***

There was fear too. I received a voicemail message later in the month. "OK, Mark, if you could please call me, I would appreciate it, honey, because I'm bewildered and I'm in a fog. So if you could do that, I would appreciate it. Thank you."

I received another one a few days later. "Mark? I'm trying to get in touch with you; I don't know what the story is. So, if you can call me, I would appreciate it, honey. OK? I *think* you have my number. All right. Bye."

It started to feel nauseating. She was so lost and alone.

***

Then, seemingly out of nowhere, there would be a day that felt more upbeat.

"Welcome to my new abode," she said cheerily one day in March.

"What do you mean, Ma?"

"I just moved in today. I don't know how things got here so fast."

"You've been here for a while, Ma."

"How long have I been here?"

"About three years."

"In *this* apartment?"

"You've been in this apartment for over a year now. You used to be in one upstairs."

"Oh my god. When did I get here?"

"About three years ago, Ma."

"Huh. *How* long?"

"It's about three years now, Ma."

***

The next month, we revisited the same territory.

"What's going on, Ma?"

"Not much new. I'm in a new room."

"No, Ma, I'm sure you're in the same room you've been in."

"But they moved all my stuff in here."

"Well, you've been there for a while, actually."

"How long have I been here?"

"The room?"

"The whole building."

"It's over three years now."

"Oh, really."

(Yes, I'm afraid so.)

"How close are you?"

"I'm close, Ma. Just five or so minutes."

"Oh, good."

***

"How many kids do you have?"

   (Two. Girls.)

   "What are the girls' names?"

   "Brenna," I said, "and ..."

   "Justine."

OK, right. Got it. Give her some helpful clues, and she could sometimes gather things back. There's more in there than meets the eye, we realized, and it was important to find ways of accessing it.

***

In April, things took a turn for the worse. "Some rough times," I wrote in my notes. Mom had absolutely no memory of anything having to do with where she was living. A torrent of words spilled forth.

   "Amazing."

   "Horrifying."

   "Terrifying."

   "My, oh my."

   "Nothing, absolutely nothing."

Her memories of people were fading too.

   "Do you remember Dad?" I asked.

   "Vaguely."

   "He's been gone for some time now."

   "He died when he was very young, then?"

   "What about Rocky? Do you remember him?"

   "I remember the name."

   "So do I know my children and my grandchildren?"

Children, yes. The grandchildren were more iffy; they have to be listed, enumerated.

   "What about their ages?"

I told the ages of our kids.

   "Look at all the pleasures I could have had," she said, "if I were alive and functioning."

Oh my god. Oh my god. Those are my words this time, not hers.

***

This period of time was filled with questions—about places, people, time, and more. There was more repetition than ever, more perseveration.

"How often do you have to put up with these questions?" she asked one time.

"Pretty often, actually."

"Why don't you just tell me to shut up?"

***

As the year drew to a close, what remained most puzzling of all to her was how long she had been at Tatnuck Park, going on four years at that point.

"If I've been here four years," she asked, "why wouldn't I know where I was?"

Questions like that one were pretty hard to answer. It was better to distract her, shift the attention elsewhere. There was no need to send her into shock and disbelief. It just didn't go anywhere.

***

Things deteriorated further the following year. There was so much she couldn't remember. Even the names of my brothers and I were shaky. She needed prompts for these too: Bobby … Kenny … Mark. Fortunately, she still remembered her own name.

"I guess that's a good thing. If I get lost again, I can tell them my name."

There was less and less for her to say at this point too, and she knew it.

"So, do you get sick of this, popping by and your mother not having much to say?"

***

In late January 2010, Justine and I stopped by for a quick visit. My mother was thrilled, gazed at Justine, and smiled a big, broad smile, commenting on how beautiful she was.

"What's your name, honey?" she asked.

"You know her name, Ma!" She clearly didn't. "Do you know who this is?"

"It's your special someone," she replied knowingly (wink wink).

"What do you mean? Who do you think she is?"

"She's your girlfriend."

Justine and I looked at one another; she giggled.

"Who?!"

"Maybe I don't know the right term. Lover?"

"No, Ma, she's my daughter! Do you remember her name?"

"No."

"Well, I'll give you three choices: Kathy, Barbara, or Justine."

"Justine."

"Right! Justine!"

"But that can't be Justine. She had blond hair, and was a child. You're a woman."

"A child-woman," I said.

***

I can't recall when I began to ask this question, but I know I did. When would she forget me? *Would* she?

At the outset of another visit later that year, I greeted her with my usual, "What's up, Ma?" Casual, just checking in.

"I'm just sitting here with an empty head."

"It's not completely empty. You remember who *I* am, don't you?"

"I'll never forget you, sweetheart."

***

Apart from me, there wasn't much left.

"They don't know what to do with me here," she said.

"What are you talking about, Ma?

"I don't know where the hell I am. I don't know where I'm going. I don't know *anything*."

The problem wasn't only hers, though. "They don't know what's going on here. There's no one around, not a person."

"There *are* people around," I told her.

"So, why am I so completely alone here now, so completely lost?"

"Because you don't remember any of it. You're here every day."

"That may be," she said, "but it still doesn't help me any."

***

By April, it became radiantly clear what the problem was. "I can't remember what I can't remember."

I told her how I just wished she weren't so miserably at sea. But this wasn't the only problem.

"I'm not near anybody I love," she added.

I don't recall how I responded to that particular declaration. Was it, "Sure you are, Ma!"? Was it, "Hey, what about *me*?!" Was it, "I can't believe you just said that!"? I don't know; although I wrote down the words, it's hard gathering back what I felt at the time. What's clear, in any case, is that her feeling of confusion and loneliness and abandon was reaching something of a fever pitch. Reality was not just slipping away, it was racing, headlong, to who knows where.

***

"Where's my apartment?" she asked another time.

"You're in it."

"This building? I don't remember that. I don't live here, though."

I tried to clarify things, but it didn't work.

"Where am I in the other place?"

"There *is* no other place."

"I didn't sleep here last night. So, where am I when I'm not living here?"

"Nowhere; you're living here."

She got up from her wheelchair and stared at her bed, utterly mystified. "So, where am I living at home then?"

I tried again. But she could only respond with more questions.

"Do they serve meals here?"

"So, where was I in the other place?"

"So, why wouldn't I recognize anything?"

As I noted earlier, it used to be that she could recognize her furniture; it was stuff she'd had for years. But that had led to confusion too. What was it doing there? How did it get there, in this new apartment? It had all happened so fast. By this point, though, the furniture was new too. And it was new in a way that felt distant, menacing even. Why would I be hurled into this new place? Who *did* this to me? *What's going on here? Why am I always the last to know?*

***

The question remains: Given the near-absence of an autobiographical self, in the sense of a self at least partially aware of her own history, how might we account for the persistence of identity, albeit in the largely negative form— identity *in absentia*, as I called it earlier—in which it had become manifested? Some of what Damasio told us about the persistence of a core self is probably relevant here. Let me try briefly to supplement that view with a related set of ideas. Even when the personal dimensions of autobiographical memory are largely erased, it may be that collective, *supra*personal dimensions remain. By suprapersonal, I refer to those aspects of memory that are derived not from firsthand personal experience, but from the vast variety of secondhand sources that are folded into "my past," "my history."

I have spoken in some related work of the "narrative unconscious," which refers broadly to "those culturally rooted aspects of one's history that remain uncharted and that, consequently, have yet to be incorporated into one's story" (2002b, p. 193). And we become aware of the existence of this unconscious "during those moments when our own historical and cultural situatedness comes into view" (p. 200). I am not suggesting that my mother herself had experienced these coming-to-awareness moments, of course; that would require a level of reflective consciousness, of *historical* consciousness, that had been superseded. But it could very well be that the narrative unconscious remains operative—in evidence more to others, such as me, than to her—in situations like the one I've described in this chapter. Consider the wish that she had expressed some years before, not long after she had begun to grow confused and frustrated over her existence. "I want to be a person," she said.

It's unlikely that she would have, or could have, uttered that statement at this stage. Times had changed. But I do think that the basic dynamic remained: She seemed to have a memory, such as it was, of how to be *a* person if not this particular one. That is, she seemed to have a kind of generic idea of what being a person, and having an identity, means. The phrase I referred to earlier—"Oh, what becomes of a person"—signaled this awareness. So did her complaints about being brainless, mindless, or like a child. There was an image in view, still, of who she once was. But this image was less tied to the particulars of her past experience than to their culturally rooted and culturally fashioned schematic contours. One might say that she had a memory of the *form* of personal identity if not the content, the concrete substance.

This mode of memory seemed to surface most often in the context of exchanges with people like me and other intimates, that is, those who mattered and who, at some point in the past, had an entirely different image of who my mother was. There is little doubt that my presence could sometimes bring about this sort of lamenting, shame-laden, mode of memory. *Why wouldn't I recognize anything? Why?* Persons are supposed to be located; they're supposed to live in places they recognize and know. *Why can't I do this? Tell me, Mark, please!*

Questions such as these underscore not only the relational dimension of memory but the relational dimension of identity as well: My mother was perhaps most *not-herself*—which is, in effect, her new identity—when she was with those who had once known otherwise.

Maybe it's time for me to leave now, I thought. *She won't be any more located when I walk out the door. But she probably won't be nearly as puzzled and disturbed by it either. Out of sight, out of mind.*

***

This too would change. Her confusion and anxiety would no longer be limited to our visits but would extend well beyond us. Her dislocation was all but permanent. And she was willing to share it with just about anyone who'd listen. But that was becoming harder, way harder. Good lord, what's next?

We would learn soon enough.

CHAPTER 5

RELEASE

It was February 2010. Mom had a lot of back pain due to a compression fracture she suffered, and needed to spend some time in the hospital. She was "alert and forgetful," the nursing notes said. Things started going downhill from there. She was increasingly out of touch with reality and was becoming belligerent, difficult to contain. Her meds weren't working as they had been; everything had to be recalibrated. We were told that she needed to spend some time in the geriatric psychiatry unit at a local psychiatric hospital, where she would stay for ten days. Some notes:

> The patient has a history of progressive dementia as well as depression and agitation. She has had a number of medication trials. She had been on Risperdal and appeared to be somewhat drowsy at times; it was discontinued. She became more agitated. It was restarted at a low dose, but she was not improving. She was also recently started on Celexa with no effect so far. Noted in her records to have a number of antidepressant trials in the past which she did not tolerate including bupropion and other unidentified SSRI. The patient was not able to supply any coherent history. Most of the history was supplied by her son who is her healthcare proxy.

She also had COPD, hypertension, osteoporosis, and some other things too; it was in the notes.

> On initial evaluation, she was alert, attentive, but really not listening to questions or responding appropriately. She was very focused on how to get to the first floor, where the elevator was; denied that she was a patient in the hospital, that she was supposed to go to Clinton Hospital but insisting this was not Clinton Hospital. She was extremely anxious with very poor attention span, poor short-term memory.

Before she returned to Tatnuck Park, her notes revealed that she had been admitted for evaluation and treatment of increasing confusion with agitation, anxiety and depression. Reports from the Assisted Living staff indicate that Marian had been decompensating over a two week period. She is described as being angry and irritable. Marian does have a Dx of dementia and depression …

During the initial phase of her admission, Marian presented as alert and attentive and oriented to person only. She presented as very anxious and would ask multiple questions and unable to listen to answers due to her short attention span. Marian would frequently ask questions and when answered—she would disagree and become increasingly agitated. Her affect has been labile with periods of anxiety and depression. She does have some insight into having problems with her memory and will make statements that her "memory is gone."

Over the last several days, Marian has been somewhat calmer. [But] She remains confused and disoriented and continues to have periods when her anxiety does increase. She will ask multiple questions and is difficult to redirect—this occurs more so in the later afternoon and early evening. Marian will be discharged to Tatnuck Park ALF on 5/5/10 and will be accompanied by her son.

***

Not a good period. In fact, it was an extremely disturbing period, partly because of my mother's confusion and agitation, but also because the unit where she stayed was terrifying and served to further dislocate her. *Bedlam*, of the sort you would find, or imagine, in a horror movie. To this day, I don't know how much of this was a function of the specific place and how much was a function of the kind of place it was and the kinds of challenges any such facility would pose. What I do know—what I did know—was that as soon as her doctors could come up with the right cocktail of meds, we needed to get out of there. Mom needed to be released from that place. And she needed to be released from her misery, somehow.

For the time being, she would return to Tatnuck Park, but we knew that her stay there would be temporary. She eventually settled down somewhat, but between her increasingly fraught mind and her increasingly frail and failing body, it was clear that a change of venue was called for.

In the application for the Jewish Healthcare Center (JHC), a nursing home close by, my brother Ken wrote:

Applicant's dementia continues to regress. She is becoming too difficult for assisted living facility to manage. Short-term physical problem in Jan.-Feb. put her in hospital for a few days. Combination of dementia and physical deterioration requires supplemental help daily at this point.

This sounds about right. Beds were scarce. We hoped they could find one for her.

***

Fortunately, one was found fairly quickly. So in May 2010, Mom began her new life at the JHC. Her service program read as follows:

Marian can be verbally abusive please direct when necessary. Moderate impairment—memory loss especially of current events—may be anxious and/or agitated about memory loss, may appear to be functional on surface but detailed conversation reveals problems of withdrawal, depression, isolation, etc. Strong reminders required. Cueing or reminders needed to go to dining room to eat; order appropriate items from the menu. Marian needs clothing laid out to put on. May need cueing during the dressing process. Individual needs physical assistance with preparation of grooming materials, help with dentures, etc. Needs help brushing teeth combing hair and with dentures.

This sounds about right too. Mom was a curious mix of things back then. Maybe she always had been.

***

My mother never knew she had been moved to a nursing home. And to the best of my knowledge, she was never disturbed by her new surroundings, institutional though they were. I guess this is a good thing. Another form of dementia's tragic promise, you could say.

Am I "glad" she didn't have a blessed clue where she was? That sounds a bit strong. But it's not far from the truth. In fact, it's not far from the truth to say that, by and large, we welcomed this new phase.

What a strange thing to say about a loved one's oblivion.

***

"Oblivion" isn't quite right, but something had definitely changed. Maybe the dementia was advancing. Maybe the new cocktail of medications was working. Who knows? Whatever it was, things had become different—calmer, even pleasant at times. I'm not sure it makes sense to say that she was "pleased" with where she'd landed, nor was she displeased. Actually, neither of those words seem to apply. That's because there was only the most minimal reflective distance at this time. She was no longer taking stock of things, no longer evaluating, measuring, against some standard of normalcy. She had moved beyond seeing herself as brainless, mindless, dumb, and all the rest. In fact, she seemed to be beyond seeing herself at all. She could still talk about a pain she had, something immediate, but she couldn't—or didn't—talk about her life or her mental state.

As for how she was taking to her new environment, it went pretty well. "Whose place is this?" she would ask. Or, "Do *you* live here?" She seemed to like it too. And that was just fine. In fact, she and I would sometimes sit in her room—her "apartment," as I usually referred to it—and she'd say, "This is a *lovely* place."

"It is, isn't it?" I would respond. "It's lucky we found it."

Objectively speaking, it really wasn't all that lovely; it was a nice, clean room in a competently run institution. No more, no less. Seen from the outside, her situation looked bleak. The disease had intensified and had left her in a state of dependency and vulnerability and fragility that would have once horrified her. She needed to be taken to the bathroom. She needed to be dressed. She needed to be fed. Still, I wouldn't describe her situation as "tragic," not primarily so, anyway.

On any given day, I might have walked into the dayroom, where people sat, watched TV (or looked in its direction), had snacks, and carried out simple activities. When Mom could still see, she might turn her head my way and say something embarrassing like, "My world lights up when you walk in," or "You look great." "Handsome hunk," even. She wanted her floormates to know too. Some of them would chime in, even a bit flirtatiously. Most of them just ignored her and kept on doing whatever they were doing. I guess it's nice that she saw me this way, but it felt a little weird too. Sometimes I think I reminded her of my dad, long gone though he was. It just seemed like an unconscious overvaluation of some sort, her delight at seeing me somehow morphing into how I looked. Whatever. Better that than indifference or disgust!

Eventually, this changed too. When she lost the ability to see, or at least appeared to, she might have still said something about my being "handsome" or told Debbie and me that we looked great, even if she wasn't looking in our direction when she said these things. It was strange. If I asked, "Can you see me, Ma?" she would say that she could. If, however, I pointed toward the television and asked her if she could see it, she wouldn't even know where to look. Functionally speaking, she had become blind. But she didn't know it. So there still remained handsome and beautiful people, lovely flowers, and more. Whether she could truly see them is immaterial. On some level, she believed she could, and that's what counted most.

We wondered whether we should take her to the ophthalmologist to see whether we could address whatever portion of the problem was actually visual in nature. No, the doctor said; there's really no way of teasing apart what's brain and what's eye, and if she's not bothered by her situation, we should probably just let it be. I did wonder a bit about his perspective on the matter. Wouldn't she be that much more nourished by the world if she could actually see it in its splendor? Wouldn't she be that much more excited to see her grandchildren and loved ones if they were there before her, clear as day? Maybe, maybe not. It's hard to say, but subjecting her to laser surgery and having to help her navigate bandages and recovery posed potential problems of its own. Ultimately, we trusted the doctor's view. As it turned out, his mother was also a victim of dementia, and knowing what he did of her world, he was confident in his position, and in the end, so were we.

***

After her seeing days had passed, there she would be, slumped over in her wheelchair, eyes closed, maybe dozing. Often, I walked over and played with her hair a little without saying a word. If all went well, her eyes would crawl open and she'd smile a gap-toothed smile. "Hi, honey," she might say. If she didn't respond, I might ask, "Anybody home?" Then, hopefully, she'd know I was there.

About that gap-toothed smile—the dental situation that emerged was similar in some ways to her vision issue. My mother had "partials," denture contraptions that supplemented her natural teeth, and by the time she moved to the Jewish Healthcare Center, they frequently went missing.

"You're missing something, Ma," I said to her one time—a front tooth.

"Maybe I swallowed it."

"No, Ma; it's just that your partial's not in."

So off we marched to her room to find it. And as she and I waited outside the bathroom, which was being cleaned by one of the aides, she gave me a great big front-toothless grin, as if she were about seven.

Look, no teeth!

Those partials went missing a few times. They may have hurt her in some way. They were also a hassle to put in. Whatever the reason, she wasn't particularly fond of them, and given her soft-food diet, she didn't seem to need them either, so the issue was mainly a cosmetic one. Did it matter if my once-beautiful mother now looked more like a disheveled street person? Not to her, it didn't. It didn't matter to me either, or to Debbie or our kids. We had seen it all, and this was just another chapter. So screw it, we said, let's just let this be too. If her occasional visitors were troubled by it, as they no doubt would be, so be it.

***

Much of the time I shared with my mother during the earlier portion of this phase was spent reviewing, catching up. She asked questions about me and my life—where I lived, what I did for a living, whether I was married, whether we had any kids. Sometimes she knew all the answers, but generally not. One way or the other, some measure of relocation and reacquaintance was always needed.

"Do you buy or do you rent?" she asked one time.

(Buy.)

"Must be quite an undertaking, as a student."

"Student?"

(No, not quite.)

"So, you bought your house while you were in school?"

"You're thinking of me as younger than I am; I haven't been in school in 25 years."

She was shocked and perplexed at this declaration, but not particularly troubled.

"How old do you think I am?" I asked.

(No idea.)

"I'm 55."

"Are you *really*?! Now, that takes me aback."

"I've got a wife and kids too, by the way."

"Did you put them in bed already?"

I told her their ages.

"*What*?! Jiminy crickets! Where do these years fly to?"

"Shocking," I said in agreement.

"It is. It really is. When I think of how old *I* am, I can't believe it."

I don't think she knew how old she was in that moment, but given the news I'd just shared with her, she knew she had to be up there.

***

"When did you get married?" she asked another time.

"In October, it'll be 25 years." That's not all. "We've got a daughter who's 24."

"You're full of surprises this morning!"

(Guess so.)

"So, you married young."

"Not really. You always think I'm younger than I am. How old do you think I am, Ma?"

"I don't know."

"I'm 55."

"You're kidding. That one almost knocked me off my chair!"

***

The questions persisted. "Do you have a wife or a girlfriend?"

"A wife! We've been married 25 years, Ma!"

"You're not that old!"

"I'm 56, Ma."

"So you're married. *How* long?"

"25 years."

"How 'bout that. Offspring?"

"Two: Brenna and Justine."

"I can't think of them either. It's hard when you live so far away."

Most important in any case: "I appreciate your taking recess with Mommy."

***

Eventually, things got shakier. Sometimes she knew my name; sometimes not. What about this time? "Do you know my name?"

"Mike?"

I feign utter shock and disbelief, and try to give her some helpful hints.

"Do you remember what the hell my name is now?!" I eventually asked.

"M-a-w-k!" she said in an exaggerated New York accent, followed by a pet name from long ago: "Merkel!"

"Who am I?" I asked another time.

"My darling."

"But *who* am I?"

"My sweet one!"

At this point, I had to resort to my increasingly customary, "I'm going to give you three choices, Ma" shtick, which usually worked. But not always.

"Who are your three boys?" I asked.

"Moe, Schmoe, and Joe."

"So, which one am *I*?"

"Schmoe!"

(Gee, thanks.)

Another three-choice exercise about my name.

A clue: "It rhymes with lark."

"Park."

(Nope.)

"Dark."

(Nope.)

"Schmark."

She kissed my hand, to make me feel better, I guess.

Another time when I asked her who I was, she was up front: "I don't know," she said, "but I love you just the same."

***

This not-knowing—and knowing?—would persist in the days ahead. I suppose I should have been troubled by it. I'd often heard of that "terrible time" when those with dementia stop recognizing their loved ones, but given Mom's demeanor, I just didn't find it that disturbing. In fact, there were some truly lovely moments, especially when it came to another round of reacquaintance. One particularly moving conversation happened when I was 57. I responded to all of her questions, of course, but here, I just want to share her words, in the order they were uttered.

"So, you're my son?"

"Are you married?"

"Do you have any children?"

"And what is your name?"

"So, do you like me as a mother?"

"So, how long have I been your mother?"

"That's a long time not to know you," she said, when I told her it's been 57 years. "Wow," she added. "Look at all the time I've missed with you."

"So, do you call me Ma?"

"So, when did I get to know you?"

"So, are you nice?"

"So, do I look at you with love?"

After she received all the answers and knew the lay of the land, she could only conclude:

"I love being your mom."

"I love being your son," I said in response.

"So, it's a good match."

Indeed it is. Some of these words bring us back to an idea we encountered in the previous chapter, when I suggested that my mother seemed to have a memory of how to be a person, just not the particular one she happened to be. The exchange I just shared bespeaks much the same idea. Although she didn't seem to remember being *my* mother, she did remember what it means to be *a* mother, the kind who looks at her children with love. Is it possible that somewhere in there she knew me? Is it possible that her words "I love being your mom" were more than simply a logical conclusion? I'd like to think so, but I really don't know. And that's OK.

***

Some evidence for the logical conclusion idea emerged in the context of another exchange we had soon after.

"I don't know you," she said to me.

"Actually, you know me pretty well."

"How do I know you pretty well?"

"You gave birth to me!"

"What's your name?"

"Mark."

"So, do you love me?"

"Of course I love you! Do you love *me*?"

"I must."

Inferential love! I'll take it. It's not that I was entirely forgotten, though.

"What do you do for a living?" she asked me another time.

"I'm a professor, over at Holy Cross."

"You must know my son, Mark Freeman!"

"Who the hell do you think *I* am?!"

***

"Do you know why I'm here?"

"No."

"I'm here to see you, because you're my mother."

"Oh, baloney!"

Another time:

"I'm not your mother, am I?"

"Yeah, you are!"

"Oh, for goodness sake."

And another:

"So, who are you?"

"A close relative."

"How close?"

"As close as can be!"

"Sister? Brother?"

"No."

"Uncle?"

"So, what's your name?"

"Mark."

"Mark what?"

For some reason, I didn't record the end of that particular conversation, but I'm pretty sure she never did quite place me. I fared a bit better another time, after I'd been away for a spell.

"Who are you?"

"I'm your son."

"How many sons do I have?"

"Three."

"Who are they?"

"Robert, Kenneth, and …"

"Mark."

"Hallelujah!"

"Oh my gosh," she said. "It's good to be here with you."

I don't remember what I said in response, but I did jot down a note. "She may have missed me," I wrote.

***

Looking back, I'm not sure why I played all these guessing games with her. We did need to get reacquainted each time; that was certainly part of it. It also felt playful, and she seemed to enjoy it. Would it have been better if I'd been straighter with her? In some ways, it seems as if each of these bouts of reacquaintance confirmed just how confused she was. That's true. But I don't think she was ever disturbed by them, or felt diminished in any way.

So there I was again, the following year, asking her who I was.

"My dear cousin? Brother? Father?"

(Nope.) "Do you know yet who I am?"

"I love you."

"But do you know yet who I am?"

"My sweetheart."

"I'm your son."

"I'm your son?"

"I'm *your* son."

"Since when?"

(I answer.)

"Which one?"

"The best one." (Apologies to Bob and Ken here too. Couldn't resist.)

Was she playing too? I don't think so, but I don't know for sure.

"Say hi, Ma," I said to her another time.

"Hi, Ma," she said.

I don't know if she was messing with me on that one either. Probably not. But I wouldn't have put it past her. Part of her remained sharp and funny, even during the later years of her dementia. I was occasionally given to wonder: Is it possible she's not as far gone as people—including me, at times— assumed? Could she have been misdiagnosed? I can remember one trivia game that led to her answering, "armada," then "egret," and several other words that were pretty obscure. She could also do some witty improvisation during these games. One day the aide read, "A person who goes up and down the beach, looking for shells and pieces of wood is called ...."

"A nut!"

None of her floormates could have done any of this. Did she really belong where she was?

Through it all, yes, I think so. There was plenty of evidence of her diminishment in certain regions of her life, particularly her self-help skills. I could speak at length about those too, though the aides and nurses and doctors who worked with her knew a good deal more about it than I did. They're the ones who had to rouse her in the morning, against her will. They're the ones who had to maneuver her into the electric lift that would allow her to go to the bathroom. I saw this sort of thing sometimes too. If I were visiting during mealtime or for a snack, for instance, I'd have to feed her. There was no mistaking the depth of the difficulties she had getting on in the world. But there was much more to her than these struggles, and my family and I had the privilege of being there with her for these times too. In fact, that's where we spent most of our time with her: talking, singing, laughing, playing.

We were lucky, to be sure; most of the people on her floor weren't doing any of this. If my mother had been more like them, I probably wouldn't have written this book. There wouldn't be much reason to add another tragedy to the dementia booklist.

"Look at what dementia can be!" This is the last thing I would want to convey in these pages, if the proclamation is taken in some across-the-board way. For many people, victims of dementia and their caregivers alike, misery and sorrow are what's dominant. I don't want to offer false hope, nor do I want to skate over the misery and sorrow that often came our way. As the previous chapter, in particular, sought to show, there were many times across the course of many years when things were downright brutal—brutal enough that I can recall speaking with one of my brothers and saying: This is too much. Debbie and I are getting exhausted and burned out. We need help, now.

All of that was real, and even during the later phase that I've been addressing in this chapter, there were some awful moments.

"I don't know who I am," she complained to me one time. "I know I'm Marian Freeman, but I don't know anything else."

"Is anybody going to come and get me?" she asked another time. "How am I going to get home?"

"I don't know how to get home. I don't know where my keys are."

People would be lost too. "How are you going to find him? I don't know where he is, who he is, nothing. I don't know."

"What don't you know?"

"I can't think of the name of the school he's in. Oh my god, I don't know what to do. I don't know where to find him."

I still don't know who she was referring to, if anyone. One thing was clear, though: "It's frightening as hell," she said.

She could get critical and caustic too, just like the old days. "Whoever the chef is, he needs to take a few more classes."

When she wouldn't even consider eating the day's meal, an aide had a ready response. "Mark cooked the food," the aide said.

"OK, I'll try it." Better than that rhubarb pie story from years ago.

And sometimes, she was downright ornery. So I wouldn't want you to think it was all fun and games during the nursing home years. It wasn't. But I hope you can see why I decided not to linger there, in the hopelessness and despair. That's just not all there was to it for us, and I want you to know this other part of the story too.

***

Some of it was positively joyful, at least for a while. After watching an Olympic hockey game together, we sang a duet of the "Star-Spangled Banner," saluting the American team. Another time, I started to sing "Meshuga" (Yiddish for crazy) to the tune of "Maria" from *West Side Story*. Mom chimed right in: "I just met a man named Meshuga …" There was also the time she spontaneously started singing, "I hate to see you go, I hate to see you go," to the tune of "The Farmer in the Dell" ("Hi-ho, the derry-o …"). It was hard to leave that day. Mom and I also "jammed" sometimes. I'd lay down a rhythm, start scatting some blues, and she'd join in, doing some scatting of her own. I have a video of one especially memorable performance, when she really kicked into gear. Pretty amazing.

And then there were her birthdays, when we'd all belt out the inevitable "Happy Birthday," which once led to her own "Happy Birthday to me!" version. We brought her some of her favorite devil's food chocolate cake that day, with gooey frosting, and after every bite, she let out a long "Mmmmm." In some ways, her experience that day was like our autumn trip up the mountain. Every bite was brand new, each one as good as the last, now gone from memory. No wonder she had gained weight during those years! On a day like that, she could have gone on eating that cake as long as it was there before her.

Another day, we brought her some barbecue from one of our local haunts. "Mmmmm," she said again. "Is that good!"

She was in luck. "It ain't over yet, Ma," I told her.

"So keep it comin'!"

Will do.

For a time, we still had the occasional happy hour. One day, I made her a gin and tonic, her favorite late-afternoon cocktail. "I love you," she said. "That gin and tonic touches my heart."

Another day, I sat with her and rubbed her arm. "Yummy," she purred. Kind of like that cake and barbecue.

Even when she didn't quite know who I was, or who she was, or where she was, our being together felt reassuring and right. "What am I to you?" she asked during another visit. "Your brother? Son?"

"You mean what am *I* to *you*," I explained. "I'm your son."

"Mark?"

"You know who I am! Why else would you call me honey?"

"Because I love you."

***

There were so many times like this, so many moments when, in one way or another, Mom would proclaim her love. Many of these proclamations were directed to me. But not only me. Indeed, "If I were to characterize Mom's world during the final phase of her life," I said at the eulogy I gave following her death,

> I would speak mainly of love. Not just for her family either. I don't know that she ever knew who the people were who cared for her, certainly not by name. But she knew them by heart, by feeling; she knew they were tender, caring people, and she was grateful, often saying, "Thank you, honey" or "Thank you, sweetheart." "I wish she was my mother," one of them said to me one day. "Shana punim!" (in Yiddish, "beautiful face") another of the aides would say to her. I know she loved that too. And I know she loved all the people who dressed her and fed her and changed her and soothed her. She felt held.

> As for us, well, it sometimes seemed that she was all love, that she had become a kind of spacious heart, all open, all welcome. "You know what?" she would sometimes say. ("What?") "I love you." And if I said it first—on leaving, for instance—she'd shoot back, "I love you more." Was this really directed at me, personally? I don't know. Sometimes I thought it was, and sometimes I wasn't sure. But it really didn't matter. She still felt something, and that something was love. How fortunate. How incredible.

***

We took lots of wheelchair excursions through the parking lot over the years.

"Nice to take a stroll with you," she said one time. "It's a treat rather than a treatment." What an amazing sentence!

We might go fast, I warned her one time.

"Fast," she said, "but not half-assed!"

"Have chair, will travel!" she yelled out another day.

"How did you find me?" she would sometimes ask when I arrived at her place.

"I always find you, Ma. Should we take a little spin?"

When I arrived for a visit, we'd go to her room, or if it was a nice day, we'd go outside, take a wheel through the parking lot, or sit by a nice little garden and try to catch up as best we could. On the good days, she'd cry out, "Wheeeee!!!" like a little kid as we rolled along.

Mom had gone from not wanting to be treated like a child, to feeling like she was one, to *acting* like one! It's kind of wonderful in a way, isn't it? There was a lot she could no longer do. But she could still play. She still *wanted* to play. (Sometimes.) Going over to Mom's now, I might have said. Playtime!

Other times, especially in the later years, she often just wanted to sit outside near the flowers. There was pleasure when she felt the sun hit her face. She would let out a little moan of gratitude, or something like it, and then she would just … be. I did the same, or I at least tried. I got pretty good at it, actually. Initially, I'd get a little antsy, feel like I had to do something—go back to work, go home to take care of this or that, whatever. Life's so busy; it's hard to let it all go. But I learned to do that. I learned to cherish it too. The opportunity to sit outside with Mom on a beautiful day, doing nothing at all except being together, maybe holding her hand—what a gift! Strange to think that it's one neither of us would have received if she had remained healthy and whole.

Some of what I'm addressing here is also reminiscent of ideas we explored earlier, for instance in my mother's ecstatic response to that fall drive we took. What she experienced that day, among many others, came to her unannounced and unbidden. It too was a gift, for her, at any rate. I, on the other hand, certainly enjoyed the day but could only go so far in my appreciation; there was too much mental chatter and clutter, and too much *self*, to be released in the way she was. In a way, I had said, I envied her.

Now was different, very different, both for her and for me. For her, there would no longer be ecstatic rhapsodizing over the beauty and bounty of the world, but rather a quiet state of repose. As for me, there was no longer envy but an equally quiet state of being-with, and an appreciation of and for the moment. I would sometimes look over at her as she felt the breeze, eyes closed, face lit up by the sunshine. For her, this wasn't really "enjoyment" or "happiness," nor was it "mindfulness." No, it seemed more like a kind of mind*less*ness, a state of purely sensuous, unintentional surrender.

Had she ever been so emptied of judgment, of care? Had she ever been so *released*? I was glad for her at these times. And I was glad to be there with her, seeing, noticing, feeling.

***

As I said near the end of her eulogy,

> I don't want to paint too rosy a picture. There were still some difficult times. And eventually, she would lose much of her vitality. Music could still get to her once in a while, but less and less. And even food, even gooey chocolate, would lose its appeal. A few bites and she'd be done. No more. That's when we knew that we were in a new phase.
>
> There wasn't a whole lot we could do with her in her final days. Often, it was hard to know if she was even awake. She'd just sit in her wheelchair, rocking her head up and down, sometimes making a strange noise or spewing out what sounded like nonsense words. She could still hold our hands; she even grabbed them tight sometimes and brought them to her lips. But then she'd loosen her grip and fade away one more time. I wouldn't call those times good. But nor were they bad. They were just … times. All I could do, all any of us could do, was just take them in, be there with her, be present. This is what I found myself doing the day Rabbi Rudnick called me to let me know she'd taken a turn for the worse. In fact, I found myself coming up with a curious term for what I was doing, or at least what I was trying to do, later that day. I was trying to *memorize* her.
>
> Would that we could memorize those we love and lose. Would that we could take them in and keep them, like a favored poem or a song. But it can't be. The face of the Other is infinite, and never was that more clear than then, there. I'm sure Brenna felt something like that when she was alone with Mom the night she passed away. She was scared, she said, both to stay and to go. Debbie and I would see Mom one last time that night, after Brenna left. Her breathing was labored but steady. About ten minutes after we left to go home, she was gone.

CHAPTER 6

DEATH, DEMENTIA, AND THE FACE OF THE DIVINE

I'm going to begin this final chapter with a reference some readers may find surprising, a very brief piece that Sigmund Freud wrote in 1915 called, "On Transience."

> Not long ago I went on a summer walk through a smiling countryside in the company of a taciturn friend and of a young but already famous poet. The poet admired the beauty of the scene around us but felt no joy in it. He was disturbed by the thought that all this beauty was fated to extinction, that it would vanish when winter came, like all human beauty and all the beauty and splendor that men have created or may create. All that he would otherwise have loved and admired seemed to him to be shorn of its worth by the transience which was its doom.

> The proneness to decay of all that is beautiful and perfect can, as we know, give rise to two different impulses in the mind. The one leads to the aching despondency felt by the young poet, while the other leads to rebellion against the fact asserted. No! it is impossible that all this loveliness of Nature and Art, of the world of our sensations and of the world outside, will really fade away into nothing. It would be too senseless and too presumptuous to believe it. Somehow or other this loveliness must be able to persist and to escape all the powers of destruction.

> But this demand for immortality is a product of our wishes too unmistakable to lay claim to reality: what is painful may none the less be true. I could not see my way to dispute the transience of all things, nor could I insist upon an exception in favour of what is beautiful and perfect. But I did dispute the pessimistic poet's view that the transience of what is beautiful involves any loss in its worth.

> On the contrary, an increase! Transience value is scarcity value in time. Limitation in the possibility of an enjoyment raises the value of the enjoyment. It was incomprehensible, I declared, that the thought of

the transience of beauty should interfere with our joy in it. As regards the beauty of Nature, each time it is destroyed by winter it comes again next year, so that in relation to the length of our lives it can in fact be regarded as eternal. The beauty of the human form and face vanish forever in the course of our own lives, but their evanescence only lends them a fresh charm ...

Contrary to those who feel despondent over the fact that life is inevitably "fated to extinction," Freud insists that this very fate, this very finitude, can intensify our experience of the beauty we behold. In the pages to follow, I focus mainly on the ways in which bearing witness to my mother's life in her final years allowed theretofore unrealized dimensions of beauty to emerge. In keeping with the way I've proceeded in the preceding chapters, I don't wish to skip over or minimize aspects of her life, or mine, that were hard and painful and that stopped well short of being "beautiful." Rather, I seek to show that the transience of things and the very pain it brought in tow were the requisite conditions for such beauty to become manifest. Indeed, this becoming-manifest was a kind of revelation, with her situation, our situation, becoming by degrees a kind of crash course not only in reimagining dementia but also, and more generally, reimagining some central features of the human condition.

***

Returning briefly to Freud, consider again the final sentence of the passage I just shared with you: "The beauty of the human form and face vanish forever in the course of our own lives, but their evanescence only lends them a fresh charm."

What exactly is this "fresh charm" he's considering here? Is he talking about something "cognitive," as in, "I know this person before me is going to die sometime relatively soon. Let me appreciate her as best I can"? There can certainly be an element of this. As I expressed in her eulogy, I found myself trying to "memorize" my mother during those quiet, still final days—impossible though I knew it was. So, yes, there is this aspect of the situation. But I don't know that "beauty" quite applied in those moments. What might he have been talking about, then? Was he thinking of something more "direct," not so much an "appreciation" as a "captivation," a captivation somehow born out of and issuing from the transience he's considering? We're getting closer, I think.

***

The eulogy I gave concluded with the following words:

A couple of days after Mom left us, Debbie and I had to go buy her a dress. We weren't sure what to get her—whether it ought to be something subdued or something bright and lively.

When I wrote to some of my cronies from way back when to tell them the news about Mom, they responded with lots of wonderful words: "A great smile, gentle soul," "a beauty inside and out with a wise smile and warmth that I only wish I had one tenth of," "kind, bright, and gentle in manner," "a gentle, beautiful woman and always welcoming," "an elegant, gracious, and welcoming woman who showed incredible patience dealing with all the crap we came up with." All true. And feisty, stubborn, opinionated, amazing with words, passionate about music and dance and food and drink, and much, much more.

We bought her a dress that was purple and blue and black and white—all jazzy, the kind of dress you could dance in.

As I said earlier, difficult though these years have been, Mom's life was a gift. She helped us stop and attend and love in ways we wouldn't have had she remained healthy. For this, we really are immensely grateful. As I also said earlier, I'd like to think she got something out of it too. Small moments became large, and very precious; and even if she couldn't quite remember them, my sense, or at least my hope, is that they "took" somehow. Given her bountiful love, I'm pretty sure they did. I take a lot of consolation in that.

She—Ma, Grandma, Great Grandma, Auntie, *Marian*—was a good mother, and mother-in-law, and grandmother, and all the rest. Let's do what we can to keep her in our hearts and our souls.

***

I hope this book is helping to do that. But of course the book isn't just for those who knew my mother and loved her, it's for any and all readers who may find in her story, in *our* story, some ideas worth thinking about. I trust that some of these ideas have already become visible: the felt indignity of feeling oneself coming undone in a culture that so prizes autonomy and self-sufficiency; the capacity for an increasingly compromised self to experience an unprecedented sense of rapture in encountering the world; the persistence of one's sense of identity, even amidst the progressive deterioration of memory and the consequent experience of dislocation it brings in tow; the utterly unselfconscious way of being in the world in the later stage of the disease and the possibilities it may present for repose and release. All of this should sound familiar at this point. That, at least, is my hope.

At this juncture, I want to say a bit more about my own experience over the course of the dozen years in question, focusing especially on what I learned about my mother, about myself, and about the world, openly and attentively seen. I need to be cautious in telling this part of the story too. This isn't going to be a "Look how much I've grown!" chapter. Nor, actually, is much of it about me, personally. It's more about the large issues—psychological, social, ethical, and spiritual—that may arise when one embarks on a tortuous journey like this one. I emphasize "may." This is my own rendition of things, no one else's, and whatever arose for me may have precious little to do with others' experience. I would like to think there's *some* measure of generality in the story I've been telling. But it's a limited one, and is more about what's possible—in certain circumstances, with certain people—than what's necessary or inevitable.

Let me modify my last statement in one small but significant way. There was indeed—there *is* indeed—one dimension of this story I've been telling that warrants words like "necessary" and "inevitable." Here, of course, I'm talking about death. That's where dementia leads, necessarily and inevitably. It's where all life leads; you hardly need me to tell you that. What makes this particular instance of it telling is how my family and I bore witness to the process, being there with my mother in real time, seeing the changes underway, and knowing full well what the ending of the story would be.

But we didn't necessarily know *how* it would be. What would the years ahead be like? we sometimes wondered. They would be hard, that much we knew from the get-go. At a most basic level, this was a no-holds-barred descent, a cascade downhill. Everything we read, everything people told us, reminded us of this. So, get ready to go low. It's inevitable. Yes, that's true; it just is. But it wasn't only that. To put the matter differently, that descent, real as it surely was, wasn't only a tragic spiral downward. It was also a kind of revelatory opening into precisely that beauty of transience that Freud addresses.

It's quite possible that some of what I just said sounds absurd to some readers. Fraught with denial. Impertinent. Weird. Beauty in dementia? Beauty in death? *Come on.*

Do I need to revisit all the obvious qualifications here? Do I need to offer additional reminders of how awful it sometimes was? Do I need to share images of dreadful decay, just to let you know that I didn't miss those? If you need or want these, let me know; I can always send some along.

· ***

Here's what I can avow, which may make what I'm aiming at here slightly more comprehensible, if not palatable: Of all the people my mother encountered during those years—aside from those who cared for her, who bathed her and fed her, who put her to bed at night and woke her in the morning—I'm probably the only one who would speak of her deepening beauty throughout the years. If people were oriented toward her beauty at all, they'd describe what she was before the dementia took hold. "She was so beautiful, my sister," her elder sister Shirley would say. "I can't bear to see her like this."

Another of her sisters basically concluded that my mother was gone. "She left us a long time ago," she said. I don't want to fault them for their feelings. And visually, using the standard "aging gracefully" indicators, my mother was a far cry from what she'd been: She had missing teeth, her face looked hollowed out, her skin was all black and blue, she was confined to a wheelchair, unable to move on her own, often kind of zoned out. By all indications, she was barely there. And of course, there was the decimation of her memory, or at least of those aspects that visitors from afar so wanted to see, to recognize. All but gone. They so wanted her to be what she had been before. And she wasn't. She had become something scarily *other*, and for some, it was a terrible shock to the system.

***

I find it interesting that the idea of the "other" can be used in two quite different ways. Seen from one angle, the one I've been describing, my mother's otherness was something foreign, alien. She was precisely *not*—that is, not what she had been. Recall how she responded to the question I asked when I saw how frustrated she was becoming with her own increasingly sorry state. "What do you want, Ma?" Her answer was swift and to the point:

"I want to be a person." This speaks with painful clarity to her demotion, her very exile from personhood. What was she if not a person? She was the other, the *othered*: an object, a thing, an *It*, as Martin Buber (1970) might put it—in this case, a once-beautiful woman now saddled with dementia, compromised, ostensibly emptied of her unique being.

My mother didn't have to be a non-person, though; she didn't have to be othered in that way. She could be de-othered, as it were, precisely by recognizing and affirming her own otherness, her own ownness, as someone "essentially other than myself," as Buber (1965) put it, someone "that does not have merely a different mind, or way of thinking or feeling, or a different conviction or attitude, but has also a different perception of the world, a different recognition and order of meaning, a different touch from the regions of existence, a different faith, a different soil" (pp. 61–62).

It took me some time to get there. Actually, I'm not sure what "getting there" could even mean. Beholding the other in her otherness without my own needs and wishes intruding? A worthy ideal. But I repeat: easier said than done. The force of the ego is strong. And decay and death still remain, for many of us—actually all of us, I think, to a greater or lesser degree—alien, and frequently threatening, scary territory. Better to avoid it entirely, some would say. That's certainly what some people in my mother's life saw: no beauty there, only decay and death, only a faceless It. No wonder my mother wanted to be a person. Even in her own eyes, I suggested, she had been demoted, exiled.

I was certainly part of the reason she felt that way. Sometimes it took the form of my correcting her, setting the record straight, pointless though it was. She was wrong. I was right. And for a time, I had to let her know.

Sometimes it took the form of frustration and annoyance, especially about her incessant repetition of observations or questions.

Sometimes it took the form of becoming maddened by her refusal to believe that my wife, my brothers, or I ever came to see her, or for that matter, cared for her at all. In situations like these, we'd try to set the record straight, then get frustrated, annoyed, and angry. And then we'd feel completely ashamed for being unable to respond in any way other than this crudely reactive way.

Like her sisters and others, I suppose I just wanted her to be other than who she'd become; I too wanted her to be the smart, vibrant, attractive woman she had once been. We all wanted to freeze her in time—which is to say, we refused to let her own decay and death enter our lives. There is a correlation here, and it's a telling one: Our refusal to see her and to affirm her in her otherness, her difference, seems to have something to do with the denial of death. Something would therefore have to change. There was the need to accept her inevitable descent and decline, her transience. Only this, it seemed, would allow, could allow, a measure of beauty to surface.

Just to be clear about the process I'm describing here, it wasn't as if I somehow made a decision to allow death to enter—as in, "Unless I begin to think differently about death, this is going to be one awful ride." Nor did I rely on some newly articulated ethical or moral principle that would allow me to see the error of my ways and the direction of its correction— as in, "It's imperative that I treat this fragile, vulnerable person better, for she's still a person and deserves it." No, what ultimately happened was quite different and more in keeping with the work of Emmanuel Levinas, whom I introduced in the first chapter, but also that of Simone Weil, and Iris Murdoch, both of whom we've also met along the way. I thank them all, from the bottom of my heart, not only because they helped me make sense of things in such a way that I could discuss them in a book like this one, but because they helped me make sense of things as they were actually unfolding in our lives at the time.

In Levinas's (1999a) terms, I eventually became my mother's hostage. I would be there for her, captivated and captive, called by her cry. "The relationship where the I encounters the You," Levinas writes, "is the original place and circumstance of the ethical coming. The ethical fact owes nothing to values; it is values that owe everything to the ethical fact" (p. 147). The Other comes before me: "The notion of the face imposes itself here .... It commands a thinking that is older and more awakened than knowledge or experience" (p. 160).

In some ways, I underwent something of an ethical shift that's in keeping with the distinction Levinas is making here. In the early years of my mother's dementia, I related to her more in terms of scripted and somewhat superficial obligations than authentic, ethical demands. I ought to go see her because that's what I'm supposed to do, I'd think. Or because I want to be a good son. Eventually, though, this would change; rather than continue to follow these banal scripts, I followed *her*—her lead, you could say. So it is that Levinas (1999a) speaks of the "extreme urgency of the commandment ... an urgency by which the imperative is, 'dropping all other business'" (pp. 33–34).

This sounds severe, as do many of Levinas's musings on our responsibility to and for others. In addition to words like "hostage" and "commandment," we encounter words like "order," "obedience," and "summons." What shall we make of them? There was indeed a phase of my mother's dementia when these sorts of words acquired a very concrete urgency, when I was literally "summoned" to her. This was when she would experience those existential "dislocations," I called them, in which she would find herself unable to determine where—or who—she was. Beyond these quite concrete summons, there was also the broader ethical summons about which Levinas speaks: drop all other business; be there; she comes first.

What we are considering here is what I have been referring to as "the priority of the Other" (Freeman, 2014a). As I confessed in a recent piece I wrote, I think I was a better person when my mother was alive. Sure, I can be hostage to my wife or my daughters or my friends or my new grandson, but with my mother, my being there for her had become a practice, a discipline. When I would go see her, she was the priority, through and through. Now that she's gone, some of that priority—and beauty—is gone too.

It's strange and somewhat tragic to think that we might require extreme circumstances, like dying mothers with dementia, to become the hostages about which Levinas speaks. But it may be so.

***

Simone Weil's work is useful in this context too. "In the beauty of the world," Weil writes, "brute necessity becomes an object of love. What is more beautiful than the action of gravity on the fugitive folds of the sea waves, or on the almost eternal folds of the mountains"—or on the folds of the mottled and bruised skin of an old woman? "The sea is not less beautiful in our eyes because we know that sometimes ships are wrecked by it," Weil continues.

> On the contrary, this adds to its beauty. If it altered the movement of its waves to spare a boat, it would be a creature gifted with discernment and choice and not this fluid, perfectly obedient to every external pressure. It is this perfect obedience that constitutes the sea's beauty. All the horrors produced in this world are like the folds imposed upon the waves by gravity. That is why they contain an element of beauty. (1951/1973, pp. 128–129)

For Weil, not unlike Levinas, we find the language of obedience. This applies not just to ocean waves and the like, but, also not unlike Levinas, to our relations with others. A key idea for her in this context is the idea of attention, undivided, drop-your-business attention, an attention fundamentally divested of self, of ego.

The effort that brings a soul to salvation is like the effort of looking or of listening; it is the kind of effort by which a fiancée accepts her lover. It is an act of attention and consent; where what language designates as will is something suggestive of muscular effort.

The will is on the level of the natural part of the soul. The right use of the will is a condition of salvation, necessary no doubt but remote, inferior, very subordinate and purely negative. The weeds are pulled up by the muscular effort of the peasant, but only sun and water can make the corn grow. The will cannot produce any good in the soul.

Efforts of the will are only in their right place for carrying out definite obligations. Wherever there is no strict obligation we must follow either our natural inclination or our vocation, that is to say God's command. Actions prompted by our inclination clearly do not involve an effort of will. In our acts of obedience to God we are passive; whatever difficulties we have to surmount, however great our activity may appear to be, there is nothing analogous to muscular effort; there is only waiting, attention, silence, immobility, constant through suffering and joy. (pp. 193–194)

In sum: To live the priority of the Other requires a kind of self-emptying, a giving-oneself-over to the otherness of the other person. The person in question "accepts to be diminished by concentrating on an expenditure of energy, which will not extend his own power but will only give existence to a being other than himself, who will exist independently of him." In this process of "transporting" oneself in this way, "one consents(s) to affliction oneself, that is to say to the destruction of oneself. It is to deny oneself. In denying oneself, one becomes capable under God of establishing someone else by a creative affirmation. One gives oneself in ransom for the other" (pp. 147–148).

Ransom for the other: another provocative metaphor, apt in its way.

***

Let me continue with a few additional words from Weil. "The love of the order and beauty of the world is thus the complement of the love of our neighbor" (p. 158). Here is a nice statement of her position:

It proceeds from the same renunciation, the renunciation that is an image of the creative renunciation of God. God causes this universe to exist, but he consents not to command it, although he has the power to do so. Instead, he leaves two other forces to rule in his place. On the one hand there is the blind necessity attaching to matter, including the psychic matter of the soul, and on the other the autonomy essential to thinking persons. (p. 158)

"By loving our neighbor," Weil reiterates, "we imitate the divine love which created us and all our fellows. By loving the order of the world we imitate the divine love which created this universe of which we are a part" (p. 158). But loving the world, being attentive to the world, is an immense challenge, actually. The reason:

> We live in a world of unreality and dreams. To give up our imaginary position as the center, to renounce it, not only intellectually but in the imaginative part of our soul, that means to awaken to what is real and eternal, to see the true light and hear the true silence. A transformation then takes place at the very root of our sensibility, in our immediate reception of sense impressions and psychological impressions. It is a transformation analogous to that which takes place in the dusk of evening on a road, where we suddenly discern as a tree what we had at first seen as a stooping man; or where we suddenly recognize as a rustling of leaves what we thought at first was whispering voices. We see the same colors; we hear the same sounds, but not in the same way. (p. 159)

Here, then, is one way of thinking of the beautiful: *the coming-into-being of the real*. There is a qualification, though, and it helps to account for why, eventually, I could find some measure of beauty in the situation in which my mother and I found ourselves. "The beauty of the world," Weil tells us, "is not an attribute of matter in itself." Rather, "It is a relationship of the world to our sensibility, the sensibility that depends upon the structure of our body and our soul" (p. 164). How fortunate: We are beings whose sensibility lends itself to perceiving and experiencing the beauty of the world! Not unlike what was said regarding love of neighbor, "The love of this beauty proceeds from God dwelling in our souls and goes out to God present in the universe." In this respect, "It is also like a sacrament" (p. 165).

But the beautiful about which Weil is speaking here is not the beautiful we ordinarily think of when we hear the term, for it is ultimately about nothing less than the order of the world, which inevitably brings us both joy and suffering. Indeed, for Weil,

Joy and suffering are two equally precious gifts both of which must be savored to the full, each one in its purity, without trying to mix them. Through joy, the beauty of the world penetrates our soul. Through suffering it penetrates our body. We could no more become friends of God through joy alone than one becomes a ship's captain by studying books on navigation. (p. 132)

I don't know that I can go quite this far. I find it hard to say that joy and suffering are "equally precious." I also find it hard to think of savoring suffering to the full; it sounds just a bit masochistic to me (and Weil herself was known to be inclined in this direction). Most importantly, though, I find them to be largely inseparable, the one alloyed to the other. That, at least, is how it would feel when I would go visit my mother and find her huddled and alone in her wheelchair, fragile, and in her own broken way, beautiful.

Business dropped. I'm here. With you. For you.

In Murdoch's (1970) terms, I would be "unselfing" at these moments, called by necessity, obedient to what was other-than-me; and it was my mother who was the source, not me or my decisions or my strong principles. It wasn't about unfettered choice, and it wasn't about moral strength. Instead, it was about a kind of vulnerable welcome, in which, by degrees, I came to see and feel the beauty that was there. For Murdoch, this process is inseparable from the idea of freedom, deeply defined and conceived. "Freedom," she writes, "is not the sudden jumping of the isolated will in and out of an impersonal logical complex, it is a function of the progressive attempt to see a particular object clearly" (p. 23), and it involves "a process of deepening or complicating, a process of learning, a progress" (p. 31). Inspired by Weil, Murdoch also underscores the centrality of attention, and with this attention, once again, comes a kind of necessity and, in turn, obedience. "This is something of which saints speak and which any artist will readily understand. The idea of a patient, loving regard, directed upon a person, a thing, a situation, presents the will not as unimpeded movement but as something very much more like 'obedience'" (p. 40). And this process is, in the end, "an exercise in love" (p. 41).

***

So far, we've explored the beholder's share and the critical role attention plays in progressively discerning reality. This is certainly a large part of the equation we're working toward here. The other large part is the nature and quality of reality itself, especially as manifested in works of art. According to Murdoch, "The chief enemy of excellence in morality (and also in art) is personal fantasy: the tissue of self-aggrandizing and consoling wishes and dreams which prevents one from seeing what is there outside one." Along these lines, "We can see in mediocre art, where perhaps it is even more clearly seen than in mediocre conduct, the intrusion of fantasy, the assertion of self, the dimming of any reflection of the real world" (pp. 57–58). Indeed, she continues, "Art presents the most comprehensible examples of the almost irresistible human tendency to seek consolation in fantasy and also of the effort to resist this and the vision of reality which comes with success" (pp. 62–63). Success is rare and difficult: "To silence and expel self, to contemplate and delineate nature with a clear eye, is not easy and demands a moral discipline." Along the lines being drawn, "the greatest art is 'impersonal' because it shows us the world, our world and not another one, with a clarity which startles and delights us simply because we are not used to looking at the real world at all" (p. 63). Moreover, "great art teaches us how real things can be looked at and loved without being seized and used, without being appropriated into the greedy organism of the self" (p. 65).

Now what, you may be asking, does all this have to do with my mother, the idea of beauty, and art? Just as great art can serve to disarm the self's egocentric energies, so too can the frail, dying person before me, the person whose demise is a reality that cannot be sidestepped, cannot be elided, at least for those of us willing and able to see and feel. One might say that there is a kind of insistence in the dying person, a demand and a command, rooted in inevitability, necessity. This is no doubt true whether the dying person before us is relatively healthy or ridden with a malady like dementia: the preciousness of transience. But add a malady of the sort to which my mother succumbed and there is, or at least can be, a marked intensification of this preciousness. And the reason, I think, has something to do with the very otherness and alienness I spoke about earlier, the one that frightened people and turned them away. What was for them a palpable ugliness was for some of us a kind of beauty: the beauty of nature, stark and real. What a gift it was to be present, literally and figuratively, to my mother's changing face, with its creases and folds, its caverns and abysses, its profound thereness, not to be sidestepped or elided but to be *seen*.

Brutal.

And beautiful.

***

For Murdoch (1970), there is a vital connection between seeing and loving. "If," she writes, "still led by the clue of art, we ask further questions about the faculty which is supposed to relate us to what is real and thus bring us to what is good, the idea of compassion or love will naturally be suggested" (pp. 64–65). The two are in her view of a piece: "It is in the capacity to love, that is to see, that the liberation of the soul from fantasy exists" (p. 65).

In speaking of fantasy, it should be noted, Murdoch has in mind not flights of the imagination and the like, but "the proliferation of blinding self-centred aims and images," which she considers "a powerful system of energy"— "centripetal" energy, as I've called it in some of my own work. "What counteracts the system," she goes on to say, "is attention to reality inspired by, consisting of, love"—"centrifugal" energy, as it were, in which "the direction of attention is, contrary to nature, outward, away from self" (p. 65). However powerful the centripetal system may be, therefore, it can in fact be counteracted, as Murdoch has put it, by attentive care, drawn forth by the Other. It would be stretching things to compare Mom to a great work of art, but her presence did perform a similar function. Just as the great work of art "shows us the world, our world and not another one, with a clarity which startles and delights us simply because we are not used to looking at the real world at all," my mother's presence—her "face"—did much the same thing. It could be like seeing reality for the very first time, and even if I weren't quite "delighted" by that, I was certainly captivated and moved. Oh, what becomes of a person!

Let's see. Let's feel.

***

When Justine (of incredible posture fame) was younger, she used to say that she didn't like being around old people. Their alienness scared her; that's probably the simplest way of putting it. As you know, though, she got a job waiting tables at Tatnuck Park, and in relatively short order, not only did their alienness and her fear diminish, but she came to love the people she served (most of them, anyway). In some ways, I went through a similar process. When I initially went to the Jewish Healthcare Center and saw all of her floormates—so damaged and broken, screaming or crying or just kind of there, barely alive, or so it seemed—I sometimes found myself asking, *What's the point?* I sometimes thought that of my mother too. And I have little doubt that, had she known what she would eventually become, she would have asked this question herself. The reason, I think, is that it's difficult to see phenomena like dementia as anything other than loss, decay, "ugly." Operating with the usual standards of vitality and beauty, this stands to reason. But it's precisely these standards that need to be challenged and overturned.

It can't be done through some sort of willful change of heart; the centripetal system is too powerful for that. It takes time, waiting, as Weil had put it, "waiting, attention, silence, immobility, constant through suffering and joy." Indeed. It's worth the wait. At least it was for us.

***

Earlier, I described what it was often like when I went over to the Jewish Healthcare Center to spend some time with my mother. Upon arriving at her place, I'd walk into the social room, where everyone sits, sometimes engaging in an activity, sometimes watching tv, whatever. My mother would likely be slumped over, half asleep, just kind of … being. All of this would change when I said hi or touched her hair or shoulder. "She" would suddenly come alive. I'm not trying to take some sort of credit for this! But there's a very real sense in which "she" really wouldn't be there, as a self, an alive and feeling person, if it hadn't been for my entry into her life at that particular moment. It nourished her. I had come to be the life-giving Other, awakening her to the world. And she would be the same for me. By degrees, I would become much more attuned to, and appreciative of, small moments together, moments of connection, grace, love.

It's possible that I'm engaging in denial when I tell the story in this way. I don't think so, though. I'm perfectly aware of what my mother could and couldn't do. Nevertheless, there were times when we would just sit together, and be with one another, in a way that was really quite wonderful—and that I'm quite sure she was aware of on some level. She wasn't relying on a "story" at this point, a narrative of the times we had shared. That requires a well-stocked memory, and a past, and some way of synthesizing things, bringing one's experiences into connection in some way. But there was still a sense that my presence meant something to her, something that somehow touched upon who she was and what she had been.

I remember one time when I told her about a talk I was about to give. After saying something about the importance of our life stories, I said, "It's also about the importance of other people in our lives. About how important you are to me, to my life. And, I like to think, how important I am to you."

"Definitely," she said.

"Sometimes people think of the self apart from others," I continued. "But a self apart from others …" I hesitated for a moment, so she completed the sentence.

"… has no existence." She might have said "is" no existence; I'm not sure. But those were her words, no lie.

As I said in the eulogy, there wasn't much we could do with Mom in her final days. This made those days that much more precious. Frustrating, in a way, too. Trying as I had to memorize her and inevitably coming up short, I found myself in a curiously ambivalent—or maybe more appropriately, *multi*valent—state. It was one part pain and suffering, suffused with loss, and another part joy and release and immense gratitude, for all that she'd been, for all that we'd shared, for all the world could be.

It was brutal.

And beautiful.

***

In some recent work (Freeman, 2020a), I have written about the "sacred beauty of finite life" and tried to draw a connection between the face of the Other and the face of the divine. I could go to my philosophical support team again to spell out what I mean by these ideas. I could turn to some of the inspiring words uttered by Levinas and the others. It's tempting. (I like a lot of those words.) Instead, though, I think it might be better at this point to just speak in my own words, as best I can. I'll put the question simply: Why "divine"?

One reason has to do with the obedience or "commandment" aspect we have considered, the idea of being "called," by necessity, to feel and to act on behalf of the Other. Here, I might just note that this being called by the Other may be every bit as fundamental or "primary" as the centripetal system Murdoch and others have spoken of. And if that's so, it suggests that we may not be, or may not primarily be, the self-seeking, egocentric organisms we're generally made out to be, but may also be "ex-centric," outward-looking and outward-seeking. Why egocentricity often wins the day and appears primary remains an important question to address. But the answer could be more complicated than is often assumed.

Another reason for invoking the language of the divine has to do with what might simply be called "revelation"—the revelation of the real. Over the course of time, and through the kind of transformation I've been describing, the world bloomed in a way, stood forth, ecstatically, became unveiled, unconcealed. Dimensions of reality theretofore obscured or unnoticed or suppressed, out of fear or oblivion or the extant standards and habits of seeing and feeling, were eventually disclosed. With this process came an intimation of unity, belonging, and *goodness* that felt, that seemed, utterly real—realer, in fact, than the more concealed world inhabited before. And it seemed to be concentrated, or seemed most visible, in the face, my mother's face, which, as I've put it before, came to acquire a kind of summoning magnetism.

Finally, for now, there was the sheer ecstatic intensity we, my family and I, sometimes felt, especially on the eve of my mother's death, when the rabbi called and we gathered together in her room at the Jewish Healthcare Center and sought to take in her final moments.

We'd had lots of extraordinary moments with my mother, moments of a sort that would not have emerged had she not fallen prey to dementia. This is worthy of a meditation on the divine in its own right: In the midst of affliction there were gifts, arriving unbidden, gifts that served to alert us to what is most precious and real. Her final moments, though, brought this to another level. We were one step closer to truly undivided, unmixed attention. And "attention, taken to its highest degree," Weil (1951/1973) suggests, "is the same thing as prayer" (p. 105). And so we prayed, and waited, silently, reverently, and *saw*. Hard seeing, I should say, at once effortful and yet, at the same time, passive, empty in a way.

Brutal.

And beautiful.

CODA

REIMAGINING DEMENTIA, REIMAGINING LIFE

Sometime after the first piece I wrote about my mother was published (Freeman, 2008a), I was contacted by someone who was compiling a volume of essays commemorating the work of A. R. Luria, the great Russian neuropsychologist. Apparently, my piece had struck a chord with this person and was seen to be in keeping with certain aspects of Luria's work. Although it had been some time since I had consulted his extraordinary neuro-biographical inquiries (e.g., 1968/1987a, 1972/1987b), my re-encounter with Luria's work allowed me to see more clearly my own debt, both to his way of thinking and his way of writing. As Luria told us, in compelling and indeed beautiful form, there is much to be learned about the human condition by exploring the sorts of brain/mind maladies that radically transform the very structure and meaning of a life. In trying to make sense of the ongoing flow of ordinary experience, there are aspects of its grounding features that will likely escape us, and because these aspects are simply "the way things are," they may go unnoticed, unheeded. But come face to face with calamitous pathologies of the sort Luria had dealt with, and the heretofore concealed may come into view.

Another, more specific feature of Luria's work that looms large in some of my own thinking and writing is his insistence on finding in memory a kind of ur-faculty, a foundational key with which some of the mysteries of mind and self may be unlocked. In *The Mind of a Mnemonist* (1968/1987a), we encounter the pathological play of a prodigious memory, and thereby discover the limits of limitlessness. In *The Man with a Shattered World* (1972/1987b), we encounter an amnesia that results not only in a time warp but a *self*-warp, a veritable deconstruction of the existential order of things. In both of these remarkable books, moreover, Luria offers an approach to depicting the human condition that finds in narrative an incomparably valuable means of getting to the heart of the issues at hand. "In this sense," Jerome Bruner (1968/1987b) writes, "Luria's humane yet naked account" of the mind of a mnemonist, is in the spirit of a Kafka or a Beckett writing of characters who are symbolically dispossessed of the power to find meaning in the world. In his way, S., Luria's patient in this book, takes his place beside Joseph K. in *The Trial*, or in the gallery of lost souls that Becket has brought to life in his stories and plays. In this new dispensation, "pathology" becomes not a domain alien to the human condition, but part of the human condition itself. Rather than dismissing the ill and the injured as beyond the pale of human explication, we ask instead about their subjective landscape, their implicit epistemology, their presuppositions. They cease being "cases" and become human beings again. And they become part of literature as well as science. (pp. x–xi)

Paul Ricoeur (1991b) has written about the idea of "narrative intelligence," which, in broad terms, refers to the capacity of the experiencing individual to make meaningful sense of his or her life through story. Along the lines being drawn here, this idea of narrative intelligence applies not only to the workings—or non-workings—of those whose lives we seek to examine, but also to the process of examination itself. Indeed, what we find in Luria's own "Romantic Science," as it's been called, is an unparalleled example of just this kind of intelligence: one that looks across the course of a life and that seeks, in its aftermath, dimensions of meaning and significance that can only emerge by telling the story of that life, or at least a portion of it.

That's what I've tried to do in this book. Personal though the journey has been, my hope is that the significance of the story told has taken readers well beyond the personal sphere. As I see it, the book is neither about my mother, nor is it about me or my relationship to her. Instead, it's about the kind of subject about whom Luria wrote: radically singular, and in that singularity, radically revealing about the human condition.

My foremost aim has been to tell it in its full measure. What might this mean?

First, I have tried to tell it in all of its dimensions, from the tragic and horrifying all the way to the comic and redemptive. This aspect—the phenomenological, broadly conceived—is primary. In speaking of my aim of telling this story in its full measure, then, I am speaking not of offering some sort of definitive, exhaustive account, but one that speaks to the full range of my mother's, and my, experience. In the present context, this meant practicing fidelity to the realities before me, which in turn meant moving beyond the somewhat more unidimensional categories of "tragedy," "comedy," and so on, and preserving what I could of the tensions and tonalities at hand through writing. The work of Luria, Oliver Sacks (1998a, 1998b), and other such neuropsychological storytellers has been an important source of inspiration for this venture. So too has the pioneering autoethnographic work of Art Bochner (e.g., 1997, 2012) and Carolyn Ellis (2009, 2018; see also Bochner & Ellis, 2016), as well as the equally pioneering work in narrative gerontology championed by Bill Randall, Gary Kenyon, and others (e.g., Randall & Kenyon, 2001; Randall & McKim, 2008; Kenyon & Randall, 1997; Kenyon, Bohlmeijer, & Randall, 2011).

Second, I have tried to tell this story in a way that's truly attentive to, and respectful of, my mother herself, *her* personhood and *her* world. This doesn't mean that I've left myself out of the picture; I couldn't even if I wanted to. But one of the things I learned through the years is how important it is to bracket my view of things and to see, and respect, hers. I might have wished that she were more cognizant of how much my family and I cared for her during the early years when she protested her condition and often felt infantilized and abandoned. I *did* wish this. I also might have wished that she could see better, or that she were more active. Or that she cared when I wasn't there. I might have wished, in other words, that she still had an existence like my own.

But she didn't.

And so, it became important to try to see her in her difference, her otherness, her own unique integrity. In this respect, one might say that there is an anthropological aspect to writing this story too. I've tried to enter this "native realm" as best I could—recognizing, of course, that my understanding of her way of being in the world was, and could only be, partial. To do this, I would learn, meant recalibrating my sense of what makes a life meaningful. It's easy for many to write off people like my mother, to exile them from personhood. But they, we, should resist that impulse, strenuously. I'll risk sounding preachy here: It's imperative to meet people where they are, no matter where they are.

Third, even as I have sought to tell this story in a way that acknowledges and respects difference, otherness, and so on, I've also sought to tell it in a way that underscores the essential humanness and dignity of the person. My mother was not an alien being, she was a *human* being, who, even amidst her myriad maladies, infirmities, and occasional oddities, displayed wonderfully human traits: humor, wit, compassion, care, love. I've tried to keep these qualities visible. I've also tried to keep visible her personhood itself. As I learned firsthand, even when the autobiographical self has all but left the scene, the person, with her unique character and way of being in the world, may remain. This came as something of a welcome surprise. Given what I knew about the connection between memory, narrative, and identity, I had assumed that moving beyond memory and narrative also meant moving beyond identity. Maybe as my mother neared the very end it was this way. But she remained recognizably herself—at least to others—well after the demise of autobiographical memory. Put in too-simple terms, she was still *there* for a good long while. It's unfortunate that those who felt she was "gone" didn't have the opportunity to see this and to feel it. Their loss.

Fourth, I've tried to tell this story in a way that allows my mother to "live on the page," and to thereby have the kind of expressive, evocative presence that we more often find in works of literature than social science. This is the aesthetic aspect of the endeavor. I'm not referring here to embellishment or ornamentation, to somehow "dressing up" the story in an overtly literary way. I'm speaking instead of the profound challenge of finding language, finding words, that might serve to open up the reality and the truth of the lives being explored. From one angle, the project is a "scientific" one, my aim being to practice fidelity to the realities at hand. From another angle, it's an "artistic" or "poetic" one, my aim being to create a picture, a portrait that lives and breathes and unconceals what is there. Writing this particular story of dementia thus leads me to what might be called "poetic science" (Freeman, 2011, 2014b). Having framed it this way, I have recently come to rethink the need for locating this sort of project under the umbrella of science (Freeman, 2015b, 2017). I have nothing against science, mind you, but I've come to wonder whether this sort of project really *is* science—however broadly conceived—and also whether there are other, more fitting ways of framing it, perhaps tied more closely to the arts and humanities (see Freeman, 2019, 2020b; Leavy, 2015, 2019; Sugarman & Martin, 2020; Teo, 2017). One way or the other, the main thing is that the book speaks the language of human experience and does so in a way that reveals its intricacies and undisclosed corridors, its messiness and its possible beauty.

Fifth, and finally—and perhaps most importantly—I've tried to offer a modest "reimagining" of dementia by highlighting some distinctive and unanticipated features of both my mother's experience and my own that seem to have gone largely unaddressed. I say "seem" here mainly because I don't know the literature well enough to say for sure. I certainly could have scoured more of it, so if there are pockets of flat-out ignorance here, I'll have to accept that. But my aim in this project has never been to become a player in the burgeoning world of dementia research and scholarship. Rather, it's been to attend carefully to experience and learn what I could from it, especially in regard to some of the central issues I've been concerned with over the course of nearly four decades: memory, identity, narrative. On the basis of what I know through work carried out by scholars such as Kitwood (1997) and Sabat (2001), there are plenty of people out there doing much more comprehensive research and theoretical exploration than what I've contributed in this book. There's also a good deal of work out there that's much more attentive to the varieties of dementia. My "N" was but a mere 1; and telling though this 1 was, there are significant limits to what I can say of a more general nature.

But enough with these qualifications. If you've gotten this far, you know what the book is and isn't. On the basis of my mother's experience during the "protest" phase, I learned a lot, not only about her as a person—how she saw herself, what she cared about, what gave her life meaning—but also her as a narrative subject, that is, a person whose very life-world was, like all of us, permeated by larger cultural narratives, "master" narratives. These larger narratives often go unrecognized; they become "naturalized," seen as the natural order of things—until extreme situations, like the one explored herein, come one's way and make them available for inspection. Valuable though this making-available may be for some in transcending or somehow overriding these narratives, for others, it seems, the naturalization runs deep and renders them all but immoveable. This is one reason my mother experienced as much pain as she did during this initial phase: Culturally constructed master narrative or not, she couldn't help but live under its spell, with the result that she felt herself to be nothing less than a non-person, a pitiful shell of what she once was and believed she ought to be still. I wish I could have helped her through this phase better than I did. The challenge was large.

On the basis of my mother's experience during the "presence" phase, I learned about some potentially salutary effects of a diminished sense of self. Although I was careful (I think) not to equate the kind of "unselfing" associated with mindfulness and meditation practices with the particular form of it brought into being by dementia, I don't want to dismiss the idea entirely. Unintentional and uncultivated though my mother's unselfing was, the effects of the process were in some ways akin to those attained through more intentional and practiced means. The inner critic is largely gone. So, behaviors that might ordinarily be kept under wraps may be more freely expressed. The "monkey-mind"—the distracted mental jumping-about that characterizes much of our experience (and that makes mindfulness as challenging as it is)—may be in abeyance too, leaving one to be more fully present to the world than is ordinarily possible. Finally, one may be so readily and fully "in the moment" that every moment is as new and engaging and, in some sense, *surprising* as the last. (What a day! [pause] What a day!) I didn't see this array of effects often; for this reason, I noted, I was unsure whether to name the phenomenon of presence as a "phase." But the effects were real, and they led me to think anew about some important aspects of the self-world relationship.

Judging by my mother's experience, these effects may be relatively short-lived. For as the disease progresses and the self diminishes further, the rapture of self-abandon may in time be replaced by either the void of indifference or the confusing rage of self-loss. I called this process "dislocation," and it certainly *was* a phase, as painful and disturbing in its own right, albeit in a different way, as the protest phase. For the most part, there was no protest during this phase, no revolt against feeling infantilized and no insistence on competence or self-sufficiency, but instead either utter perplexity or shameful avowal of diminishment: I am a child. I need to be put in a nursery. I don't have a brain anymore. Where did it go? How did I get here? When did I get here? What are all my things doing here? How long have I been here? And so on. Dislocation. Disbelief. And, eventually, profound disturbance, enough to land Mom on that geriatric psych ward, where, if all went well, she'd be able to calm down, return to "normal." Through it all, some sense of identity remained throughout this phase. She continued to say "I." And even though this "I" had little relationship to the "me" that had existed, she knew enough of what she had once been to lament its loss. Oh, my god. Oh, my god.

Some remnants of dislocation persisted into the next and final phase. There were still questions at times, similar or even identical to ones posed before, but they had a different air about them. There was virtually never outright panic during this phase, of the sort that had sometimes required me or Debbie to race over to see her, and there wasn't much confusion either. Instead, questions were often posed with an air of curiosity. Whose place is this anyway? And *who* are you? "Oh, my god" was replaced with a more complacent, "Oh …" Nice place. Nice to see you, or a more taken aback "Oh?!" You're 57? You're married, with kids?! (*Seriously*?!) The "I" would eventually be diminished, if not entirely extinguished. And with it, so too would the sense of loss and the lamentation that had derived from it. I hesitate to say it, but in some ways this phase was the "easiest" of them all. Why the hesitation? Well, Mom was more diminished than ever, physically as well as mentally, and many of the touchstones that had formerly been there were either gone or on their way out. But there was also minimal pain, virtually no boredom, and as delighted as she may have been to see me and my family, she didn't seem to miss us one bit when we weren't there. Yes, she was a far cry from who and what she had been. I suppose that's reason for some grief on our part. But just as she no longer felt loss, neither, for the most part, did we.

Everything had shifted. Our expectations had gotten ratcheted down, along with our hopes and wishes. Mom's situation was hopeless, but not in the way that seemingly despairing word ordinarily connotes. Maybe hopeless isn't the right word. Hope-free? Future-free? In some ways, we all ended up living in the moment during this phase, particularly toward the end. Nothing was more important, nothing was more necessary, than just being there, together, breathing in the bittersweet air of life, and eventually, death.

Mom died just after the stroke of midnight on the Sabbath. In keeping with Jewish tradition, this meant that she would have to be kept in her room until sundown the next day, when she would be moved to a funeral home. What should we do? We did what we felt at the time was the most obvious thing to do: go over to the Jewish Healthcare Center and spend some quality time with her. I don't know that I would call that day a "nice" one, but it was a beautiful one, one that we'll remember and treasure, forever.

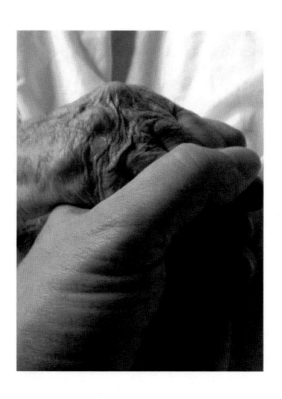

REFERENCES

Bamberg, M. (2006). Stories: Big or small: Why do we care? *Narrative Inquiry, 16*(1), 139–147.

Bamberg, M., & Georgakopolou, A. (2008). Small stories as a new perspective in narrative and identity analysis. *Text & Talk, 28*(3), 377–396.

Basting, A. D. (2009). *Forget memory: Creating better lives for people with dementia*. Johns Hopkins University Press.

Bataille, G. (1988). *Inner experience*. SUNY Press.

Benson, C. (1993). *The absorbed self: Pragmatism, psychology and aesthetic experience*. Harvester Wheatsheaf.

Bochner, A. P. (1997). It's about time: Narrative and the divided self. *Qualitative Inquiry, 3*(4), 418–438.

Bochner, A. P. (2001). Narrative's virtues. *Qualitative Inquiry, 7*(2), 131–157.

Bochner, A. P. (2012). Bird on the wire: Freeing the father within me. *Qualitative Inquiry, 18*(2), 168–173.

Bochner, A. P., & Ellis, C. (2016). *Evocative autoethnography: Writing lives and telling stories*. Routledge.

Bruner, J. (1987a). Life as narrative. *Social Research, 54*, 11–32.

Bruner, J. (1987b). *Foreword to the 1987 edition of A. R. Luria's The mind of a mnemonist*. Harvard University Press. (Original work published 1968)

Buber, M. (1965). *Between man and man*. Macmillan.

Buber, M. (1970). *I and thou*. Charles Scribner's and Sons.

Cohen, D., & Eisdorfer, C. (2001). *The loss of self: A family resource for the care of Alzheimer's disease and related disorders*. W.W. Norton & Company.

Csikszentmihalyi, M. (1990). *Flow: The psychology of optimal experience*. Harper Perennial.

Damasio, A. (1999). *The feeling of what happens: Body and emotion in the making of consciousness*. Harcourt, Inc.

DeBaggio, T. (2002). *Losing my mind: An intimate look at life with Alzheimer's*. Free Press.

Ellis, C. (2007). Telling secrets, revealing lives: Relational ethics in research with intimate others. *Qualitative Inquiry, 13*(1), 3–29.

Ellis, C. (2009). *Revision: Autoethnographic reflections on life and work*. Left Coast Press.

Ellis, C. (2018). *Final negotiations: A story of love, loss, and chronic illness*. Temple University Press.

Freeman, M. (1993). *Rewriting the self: History, memory, narrative*. Routledge.

Freeman, M. (1997a). Why narrative? Hermeneutics, historical understanding, and the significance of stories. *Journal of Narrative and Life History, 7*(1–4), 169–176.

Freeman, M. (1997b). Death, narrative integrity, and the radical challenge of self-understanding: A reading of Tolstoy's Death of Ivan Ilych. *Ageing and Society, 17*(4), 373–398.

Freeman, M. (1999). Culture, narrative, and the poetic construction of selfhood. *Journal of Constructivist Psychology, 12*(2), 99–116.

Freeman, M. (2000). When the story's over: Narrative foreclosure and the possibility of self-renewal. In M. Andrews, S. D. Sclater, C. Squire, & A. Treacher (Eds.), *Lines of narrative: Psychosocial perspectives* (pp. 81–91). Routledge.

Freeman, M. (2002a). The presence of what is missing: Memory, poetry, and the ride home. In R. J. Pellegrini & T. R. Sarbin (Eds.), *Between fathers and sons: Critical incident narratives in the development of men's lives* (pp. 165–176). Haworth.

Freeman, M. (2002b). Charting the narrative unconscious: Cultural memory and the challenge of autobiography. *Narrative Inquiry, 12*(1), 193–211.

Freeman, M. (2003). Data are everywhere: Narrative criticism in the literature of experience. In C. Daiute & C. Lightfoot (Eds.), *Narrative analysis: Studying the development of individuals in society* (pp. 63–81). Sage.

Freeman, M. (2004). The priority of the other: Mysticism's challenge to the legacy of the self. In J. Belzen & A. Geels (Eds.), *Mysticism: A variety of psychological approaches* (pp. 213–234). Rodopi.

Freeman, M. (2006). Life "on holiday"? In defense of big stories. *Narrative Inquiry, 16*(1), 131–138.

Freeman, M. (2008a). Beyond narrative: Dementia's tragic promise. In L.-C. Hyden & J. Brockmeier (Eds.), *Health, illness, and culture: Broken narratives* (pp. 169–184). Routledge.

Freeman, M. (2008b). Life without narrative? Autobiography, dementia, and the nature of the real. In G. O. Mazur (Ed.), *Thirty year commemoration to the life of A. R. Luria* (pp. 129–144). Semenko Foundation.

Freeman, M. (2009). The stubborn myth of identity: Dementia, memory, and the narrative unconscious. *Journal of Family Life, 1*. Retrieved March 19, 2009, from http://www.journaloffamilylife.org/mythofidentity

Freeman, M. (2010ab). Narrative foreclosure in later life: Possibilities and limits. In G. Kenyon, E. Bohlmeijer, & W. L. Randall (Eds.), *Storying later life: Issues, investigations, and interventions in narrative gerontology* (pp. 3–19). Oxford University Press.

Freeman, M. (2010b). *Hindsight: The promise and peril of looking backward.* Oxford University Press.

Freeman, M. (2010a). Narrative foreclosure in later life: Possibilities and limits. In G. Kenyon, E. Bohlmeijer, & W. L. Randall (Eds.), *Storying later life: Issues, investigations, and interventions in narrative gerontology* (pp. 3–19). Oxford University Press.

Freeman, M. (2011). Toward poetic science. *Integrative Psychological and Behavioral Science, 45*(4), 389–396.

Freeman, M. (2013). Storied persons: The "double triad" of narrative identity. In J. Martin & M. H. Bickhard (Eds.), *Contemporary perspectives in the psychology of personhood: Philosophical, historical, psychological, and narrative* (pp. 223–241). Cambridge University Press.

Freeman, M. (2014a). *The priority of the other: Thinking and living beyond the self.* Oxford University Press.

Freeman, M. (2014b). Qualitative inquiry and the self-realization of psychological science. *Qualitative Inquiry, 20*(2), 119–126.

Freeman, M. (2015a). Narrative hermeneutics. In J. Martin, J. Sugarman, & K. L. Slaney (Eds.), *The Wiley handbook of theoretical and philosophical psychology: Methods, approaches, and new directions for social sciences* (pp. 234–247). Wiley Blackwell.

Freeman, M. (2015b). Narrative psychology as science and as art. In J. Valsiner, G. Marsico, N. Chaudhary, T. Sato, & V. Dazzani (Eds.), *Psychology as a science of human being: The Yokohama Manifesto* (pp. 349–364). Springer.

Freeman, M. (2017). Narrative inquiry. In P. Leavy (Ed.), *Handbook of arts-based research* (pp. 123–140). Guilford Press.

Freeman, M. (2018). Qualitative psychology's coming of age: Are there grounds for hope? In B. Schiff (Ed.), *Situating qualitative methods in psychological science* (pp. 100–111). Routledge.

Freeman, M. (2019). Toward a poetics of the other: New directions in post-scientific psychology. In T. Teo (Ed.), *Re-envisioning theoretical psychology: Diverging ideas and practices* (pp. 1–24). Palgrave Macmillan.

Freeman, M. (2020a). The sacred beauty of finite life: Re-imagining the face of the other. *Psychoanalytic Inquiry, 40*(3), 161–172.

Freeman, M. (2020b). Psychology as literature: Narrative knowing and the project of the psychological humanities. In J. Sugarman & J. Martin (Eds.), *A humanities approach to the psychology of personhood* (pp. 30–48). Routledge.

Freud, S. (1957). On transience. *Standard Edition, 14*, 305–307. Hogarth. (Original work published 1915)

Geist, M. E. (2008). *Measure of the heart: A father's Alzheimer's, a daughter's return.* Springboard Press.

Georgakopolou, A. (2007). *Small stories, interaction and identities.* John Benjamins Publishing.

Gergen, K. J. (2009). *Relational being: Beyond self and community.* Oxford University Press.

Gergen, K. J., Josselson, R., & Freeman, M. (2015). The promises of qualitative inquiry. *American Psychologist, 70*(1), 1–9.

Gilligan, C. (1982). *In a different voice: Psychological theory and women's development.* Harvard University Press.

Guillemin, M., & Gillam, L. (2004). Ethics, reflexivity, and 'ethically important moments' in research. *Qualitative Inquiry, 10*(2), 261–280.

Hammack, P. L. (2011). Narrative and the politics of meaning. *Narrative Inquiry, 21*(2), 311–318.

Hammack, P. L., & Toolis, E. E. (2015). Putting the social into personal identity: The master narrative as root metaphor for psychological and developmental science. *Human Development, 58*(6), 350–364.

Heidegger, M. (1971). *Poetry, language, thought.* Harper Colophon.

Hughes, J. C., Louw, S. J., & Sabat, S. R. (2006). *Dementia: Mind, meaning, and the person.* Oxford University Press.

Hydén, L.-C. (2017). *Entangled narratives: Collaborative storytelling and the re-imagining of dementia.* Oxford University Press.

Hydén, L.-C., Lindemann, H., & Brockmeier, J. (2014). *Beyond loss: Dementia, identity, personhood.* Oxford University Press.

James, W. (1950). *The principles of psychology.* Dover. (Original work published 1890)

Josselson, R. (2006). The ethical attitude in narrative research. In J. Clandinin (Ed.), *Handbook of narrative inquiry: Mapping a methodology* (pp. 537–566). Sage.

Kenyon, G., Bohlmeijer, E., & Randall, W. L. (Eds.). (2011). *Storying later life: Issues, investigations, and interventions in narrative gerontology.* Oxford University Press.

Kenyon, G., & Randall, W. L. (1997). *Restorying our lives: Personal growth through autobiographical reflection.* Praeger.

Kitwood, T. (1997). *Dementia reconsidered: The person comes first.* Open University Press.

Leavy, P. (2015). *Method meets art: Arts-based research practice.* Guilford Press.

Leavy, P. (Ed.). (2019). *Handbook of arts-based research.* Guilford Press.

Levinas, E. (1985). *Ethics and infinity.* Duquesne University Press.

REFERENCES

Levinas, E. (1996a). *Proper names*. Stanford University Press.
Levinas, E. (1996b). Transcendence and height. In A. T. Peperzak, S. Critchley, & R. Bernasconi (Eds.), *Emmanuel Levinas: Basic philosophical writings* (pp. 11–31). Indiana University Press. (Original work published 1962)
Levinas, E. (1996c). Substitution. In A. T. Peperzak, S. Critchley, & R. Bernasconi (Eds.), *Emmanuel Levinas: Basic philosophical writings* (pp. 80–95). Indiana University Press. (Original work published 1962)
Levinas, E. (1996d). God and philosophy. In A. T. Peperzak, S. Critchley, & R. Bernasconi (Eds.), *Emmanuel Levinas: Basic philosophical writings* (pp. 129–148). Indiana University Press. (Original work published 1962)
Levinas, E. (1999a). *Alterity and transcendence*. Columbia University Press.
Levinas, E. (1999b). *Of God who comes to mind*. Stanford University Press.
Lopate, P. (2013). *To show and to tell: The craft of literary nonfiction*. The Free Press.
Luria, A. R. (1987a). *The mind of a mnemonist*. Harvard University Press. (Original work published 1968)
Luria, A. R. (1987b). *The man with a shattered world*. Harvard University Press. (Original work published 1972)
McAdams, D. P. (1997). *The stories we live by: Personal myths and the making of the self*. Guilford Press.
McAdams, D. P., Josselson, R., & Lieblich, A. (Eds.). (2006). *Identity and story: Creating self in narrative*. American Psychological Association.
McAdams, D. P., & McLean, K. C. (2013). Narrative identity. *Current directions in psychological science, 22*(3), 233–238.
Miller, S. (2003). *The story of my father: A memoir*. Bloomsbury.
Murdoch, I. (1970). *The sovereignty of good*. Routledge.
Noddings, N. (1984). *Caring: A feminine approach to ethics and moral education*. University of California Press.
Randall, W. L., & Kenyon, G. (2001). *Ordinary wisdom: Biographical aging and the journey of life*. Praeger.
Randall, W. L., & McKim, E. (2008). *Reading our lives: The poetics of growing old*. Oxford University Press.
Ricoeur, P. (1991a). Life in quest of narrative. In D. Wood (Ed.), *On Paul Ricoeur: Narrative and interpretation* (pp. 20–33). Routledge.
Ricoeur, P. (1991b). Life: A story in search of a narrator. In M. Valdés (Ed.), *A Ricoeur reader: Reflection and imagination* (pp. 425–437). University of Toronto Press.
Ricoeur, P. (1992). *Oneself as another*. University of Chicago Press.
Sabat, S. R. (2001). *The experience of Alzheimer's disease: Life through a tangled veil*. Blackwell.
Sacks, O. (1998a). *The man who mistook his wife for a hat and other clinical tales*. Touchstone.
Sacks, O. (1998b). *A leg to stand on*. Touchstone.
Sartwell, C. (2000). *End of story: Toward an annihilation of language and history*. SUNY.
Schiff, B. (2018). *A new narrative for psychology*. Oxford University Press.
Skloot, F. (2004). *In the shadow of memory*. University of Nebraska Press.
Strawson, G. (2004). Against narrativity. *Ratio, 17*(4), 428–452.
Sugarman, J., & Martin, J. (Eds.). (2020). *A humanities approach to the psychology of personhood*. Routledge.

Teo, T. (2017). From psychological science to the psychological humanities: Building a general theory of subjectivity. *Review of General Psychology, 21*(4), 281–291.

Weil, S. (1973). *Waiting for God*. Harper & Row. (Original work published 1951)

Weil, S. (1997). *Gravity and grace*. Routledge. (Original work published 1952)

Whouley, K. (2011). *Remembering the music, forgetting the words: Travels with mom in the land of dementia*. Beacon Press.

ABOUT THE AUTHOR

Mark Freeman received his Ph.D. from the Committee on Human Development at the University of Chicago in 1986, and is Distinguished Professor of Ethics and Society and Professor of Psychology in the Department of Psychology at the College of the Holy Cross in Worcester, Massachusetts. His writings include *Rewriting the Self: History, Memory, Narrative* (winner of the Alpha Sigma Nu National Book Award in 1994); *Finding the Muse: A Sociopsychological Inquiry into the Conditions of Artistic Creativity* (designated an Outstanding Academic Book by *Choice* magazine in 1995); *Hindsight: The Promise and Peril of Looking Backward* (Oxford, 2010); *The Priority of the Other: Thinking and Living Beyond the Self* (Oxford, 2014); and numerous articles and chapters on issues ranging from memory and identity to the psychology of art and religion. Recipient of the 2010 Theodore R. Sarbin Award as well as the Steve Harrist Distinguished Service Award in the Society for Theoretical and Philosophical Psychology, Freeman is also a Fellow in the American Psychological Association, has served as past President of the Society for Qualitative Inquiry in Psychology and the Society for Theoretical and Philosophical Psychology, and currently serves as editor for the Oxford University Press series, "Explorations in Narrative Psychology."

Freeman and his family—his wife Debbie, daughters Brenna and Justine, son-in-law Matt, and grandson Shaun—all live in Worcester, which they are happy to call home. Alongside his many writing projects, Freeman is a cyclist, a guitarist, a world traveler, a lover of good food and drink, and considers himself extremely fortunate to have a loving family and many long-lasting friendships, some of which date all the way back to elementary school. He and his family are also fortunate to have had Mom/Grandma close by for the final years of her life.

Made in the USA
Columbia, SC
02 April 2022

58411778R00084